THE INFLUENCE OF PETER

A verse-by-verse study of I and II Peter

By Dr. Dino Pedrone

PRESS

The Influence of Peter
A synopsis of Peter's life and verse-by-verse study of I and II
by Dr. Dino Pedrone

Printed in the United States of America

ISBN 9781624193583

Unless otherwise indicated, Bible quotations are taken from The King James Version and The New King James Version of the Bible. NKJV. Copyright © 1982 by Thomas Nelson, Inc. Used by permission.

www.xulonpress.com

Table of Contents

DEDICATION

To my dear friends
The Board of Trustees
Davis College

Dan Babcock,
Business Leader, Binghamton,
New York
Thanks, Dan, for your vision,
entrepreneurial leadership, and
friendship

Ken Barber,
Businessman, Binghamton,
New York
Thanks, Ken, for your godly
wisdom, understanding and support

Dan Campbell,
Copartner Capin and Crouse,
Atlanta, Georgia
Thanks, Dan, for your incites,
understanding, and expertise to our
college

Barbara King, Esq.,
Attorney, Albany, New York
Thanks, Barbara, for your guidance
in legal issues and your sweet spirit

T.E. Koshy, Ph.D.,
International Speaker, Chaplain,
Syracuse, New York
Thanks, T.E., for your international
influence that has caused changes to
thousands of lives for the Kingdom

"Scotty" James Little, M.D.,
Stearns, Kentucky
Thanks, Scotty, for your
unswerving allegiance to God's
Kingdom and your influence on
Davis College

Jan Chandler,
Ministry to college students, Ithaca, New York
Thanks, Jan, for being a prayer warrior and your love for students

Jeff Coghlan,
Business Leader, Binghamton, New York
Thanks, Jeff, for your giving heart, vision, and incredible leadership

Keli Cooper,
Business Leader, Binghamton, New York
Thanks, Keli, for your leadership, heart, and being there for so many students

Bill Dykes,
Christian Leader, Maineville, Ohio
Thanks, Bill, for your connecting the college with so many professionals and your friendship

Rudy Holland, D.D,
Pastor, Sanford, North Carolina
Thanks, Rudy, for being a friend, brother, and the love you express to Davis

Mike Houlihan,
Businessman, Pastor, Fort Lauderdale, Florida
Thanks Mike, for your prayer life and commitment to the word of God

Solomon Massey,
Financial Planner, Businessman, Syracuse, New York
Thanks, Solomon, for your expert advice, Godly comeraderie, and your love for Davis College

Brian Mentzer,
Pastor, Leader, Upper Marlboro, Maryland
Thanks, Brian, for being a leader among leaders

Larry Reesor, D.D.,
International Leader, Acwroth, Georgia
Thanks, Larry, for teaching us how to effectively reach the world with the gospel

Mike Sanders,
Pastor, Chambersburg, Pennsylvania
Thanks, Mike, for carrying the torch of Davis College in an incredible way!

Gary Smith, D.Ed.,
Educator, Binghamton, New York
Thanks, Gary, for your educational advice and leadership in a College of Biblical higher education

Jim Walter,
Pastor, Little Meadows, Pennsylvania
Thanks, Jim, for being a pastor's pastor and adviser to our college for many years

INTRODUCTION

$\mathcal{T}$here are certain historical characters I wish I knew personally. One such individual is the Apostle Peter. He appears to be the epitome of the sanguine personality – emotionally up one moment and down the next. He is a most unique person. I visualize him as the third-grade student raising his hand to every question posed by the instructor. He probably does not know many answers but he does want to be noticed and lacks no confidence.

We are introduced to the man when Jesus is walking by the Sea of Galilee. He sees Peter and his brother Andrew. The word from the Lord was simple and direct. Peter liked it that way. *"Follow me and I will make you fishers of men"* (Mt. 4:19). Both men immediately left their nets and followed Him (Mt. 4:20). He is later listed in Mt. 10:2, *"Now the names of the twelve apostles are these: first Simon who is called Peter. . ."* Peter liked to be first!

It was this sanguine, believing disciple who told Jesus to *". . .command me to come to you on the water"* (Mt. 14:28). The terrified disciples heard Jesus announce that He is the ghostlike figure, in the midst of the storm, walking on the water. Peter steps out of the boat, walks on the water to Jesus, and does well as he heads toward his Rabbi. He takes his eyes off Jesus and sees the boisterous waves and cries, *"Lord, save me"* (Mt. 4:30).

The disciples began to understand that the teachings of Jesus were offensive to religious leaders. In one such discussion Jesus was explaining that what defiled someone was what came out of their mouth, not what went in (Mt. 15:10-14). Jesus gave a brief explanation by utilizing His typical source of teaching (the use of a parable). Perhaps the disciples did not understand the Lord's teaching. It was, as usual, Peter who said *". . .explain this parable to us"* (Mt. 15:15). As I look at this passage it seems to me that Peter is saying "what are you talking about" or "what do you mean by this?" Peter was quick to say what was on his mind. Often he did it with deep purpose, but at other times he did it with little thought. But Peter's concept was, "I must be heard!"

Perhaps his greatest moment was at a place known today as Banias. It is the region of Caesarea Philippi. Jesus had been there teaching His disciples; as they traveled, they often learned. There were regular conversations, discussions, and teachings with the disciples. Now in true rabbinical form, a question was asked: *"Who do men say, that I, the Son of man, am?"* This was test day! This was the mega exam. Several disciples preempted Peter and listed various key individuals of biblical history. The forerunner of Jesus, John the Baptist, is mentioned. The prophet Elijah is mentioned; he was taken to Heaven in a whirlwind. The weeping prophet, Jeremiah is also a possibility. The responses were perhaps solicited by the disciples from others as they traveled with Jesus. Peter could not contain himself; He has the answer. He is ready to leap out of his skin! *"You are the Christ, the son of the Living God"* (Mt. 16:16). The Christ means the anointed one. He is the Messiah. Jesus is not just the Son of man, but the Son of God. He is the Messiah. Peter got it!

It was from the basis of this truth that Jesus began His journey to die for the sins of the world. God had become a man and therefore qualified to be mankind's redeemer. Jesus told Peter that the Father in Heaven revealed this to him (Mt. 16:17)! The rock of salvation would be Jesus. Even the gates of Hell themselves could not stop the plan of Jesus going to the cross. It was now that Jesus would begin to identify His purpose on the earth. *"From that time Jesus began to show His disciples that He must go to Jerusalem, and suffer. . ., and be killed, and be raised the third day"* (Mt. 16:21).

The event at Banias and the next conversation does not have a timeline but immediately after in the sequence of Scripture, Peter, who has made the epoch statement about Jesus, tells him, *"far be it from you, Lord: this shall not happen to you!"* (Mt. 16:22). Jesus is the Christ. He is the Messiah! He is God and has a key purpose that is so important! Peter was on target about who Jesus was! But he completely missed about what Jesus came to do. Jesus, who just said, *"Blessed are you Simon. . ."* now states to Peter, *"Get behind me, Satan! You are an offense to me, for you are not mindful of the things of God, but the things of men"* (Mt. 16:23). In fairness to Peter, the other disciples did not grasp this truth either.

Peter was in the inner circle. He was a part of the threesome closest to Jesus. They were chosen to go to a high mountain with their Lord and the amazing story of the transfiguration took place there. Peter, James, and John all saw their Lord transfigured. Jesus was in beautiful clothes, white as light and His face was shining as the sun. Then Moses and Elijah appear! What a sight! True to his personality, Peter has what he considers a great idea! *"Lord, it is good for us to be here: if you wish let us make here three tabernacles; one for you, one for Moses, and one for Elijah"* (Mt. 17:4). The Kingdom is not about buildings! As Peter spoke, he was full of fear, then a bright cloud overshadowed them and the Father from Heaven said, "This is my beloved Son, in whom I am well pleased, hear Him!" Peter once again considered a plan to recommend to Jesus. The purpose of the transfiguration was to reveal more than just who Jesus was but also His plan, *". . .likewise the Son of man is about to suffer in their hands"* (Mt. 17:12b).

It is also interesting that it was Peter who posed a key question about forgiveness. *"Lord, how often shall my brother sin against me, and I forgive him? Up to seven times?"* (Mt. 18:21). Jesus' remarkable teaching aided Peter on how God practices forgiveness.

Then Peter came to Him and said, "Lord, how often shall my brother sin against me, and I forgive him? Up to seven times?"

Jesus said to him, "I do not say to you, up to seven times, but up to seventy times seven. Therefore the kingdom of heaven is like a certain king who wanted to settle accounts with his servants. And when he had begun to settle accounts, one was brought to him who owed him ten thousand talents. But as he was not able to pay, his master commanded that he be sold, with his wife and children and all that he had, and that payment be made. The servant therefore fell down before him, saying, 'Master, have patience with me, and I will pay you all.' Then the master of that servant was moved with compassion, released him, and forgave him the debt.

"But that servant went out and found one of his fellow servants who owed him a hundred denarii; and he laid hands on him and took him by the throat, saying, 'Pay me what you owe!' So his fellow servant fell down at his feet and begged him, saying, 'Have patience with me, and I will pay you all.' And he would not, but went and threw him into prison till he should pay the debt. So when his fellow servants saw what had been done, they were very grieved, and came and told their master all that had been done.

Then his master, after he had called him, said to him, 'You wicked servant! I forgave you all that debt because you begged me. Should you not also have had compassion on your fellow servant, just as I had pity on you?' And his master was angry, and delivered him to the torturers until he should pay all that was due to him. "So My heavenly Father also will do to you if each of you, from his heart, does not forgive his brother his trespasses" (Mt. 18:21-35).

Peter's ministry was to take a downward spiral. In the garden before the crucifixion, Jesus was in deep prayer with His disciples, the inner three, the close associates that included Peter. As Jesus prayed, the three slept. Then the soldiers arrived. Even though he was sleeping when he should have been praying, it was Peter who was ready to fight. Peter drew his sword and began swinging. He cut off Malchus' ear (Mk. 14:46-47). Peter said ". . .*even if everyone runs away because of you, I will never run away"* (Mt. 26:33 HCSB). Then the pressure began to build as the apostles watch Jesus being led away. The Apostle John evidently has a relationship with the high priest and walks towards the palace. Peter accompanies his friend,

John. There the unthinkable happens: three times Peter is accused of being with Jesus. In the midst of a fear that gripes his soul, Peter curses and denies the Savior, placing on Jesus the ultimate disparity ". . .*I don't know the man*" (Mt. 26:72). Peter's accent and the fact that there were those who saw him with Jesus leave little doubt in anyone's mind. "He was one of them," the opposition states. Peter denounces any knowledge of Jesus altogether.

There is an old joke that goes like this, "When I was twenty I was concerned what people thought about me; when I turned sixty, I realized no one was thinking about me!" To deny Jesus is one thing, but to state no knowledge of Him is the apex of humiliation. Peter saw Jesus turn and look at him (Luke 22:61). This brave, sanguine personality is in absolute despair. Peter has blown it. He would never forget that look. His life with his rabbi, the Son of God, the Rock, is now over. Here is an interesting contrast: Judas, in his despair, chose suicide. Peter in despair chooses to go back to the way things were. His dreams of the kingdom are dashed. His life has been a deceptive ideology of failure. And what makes it a complete disaster is that He told Jesus he would be with Him and fight for Him. Now, when Jesus needed him, he has not only forsaken Him, but denied he even knew Him! Peter wept bitterly (Mt. 26:75; Mk. 14:72; Luke 23:62).

When Jesus rose from the grave He first appeared to Mary Magdalene. She ran to tell Peter and John. The apostles raced to the empty tomb and find that the stone is rolled back. John arrived first and looks in. Then Peter arrived and walked into the tomb. He saw something that will stay with him forever – the napkin that was wrapped around Jesus' head. It was now folded in a location sepa-rate from the rest of the linen clothes. Peter knew Jewish custom. He understood the reality and symbolism of the folded napkin. I can almost see a smile begin on his face. When royalty ate a large meal, they would often rise from their couch and walk in the garden. If they took the napkin, wiped their mouth and waded it up, it meant they were done and would not return to eat. If the napkin was folded at their seat, it meant they were coming back. Peter saw the napkin. Someone had folded it and put it there. Immediately he realized that Jesus was alive! He was coming back! John then enters the tomb and also believes. Shortly thereafter, Jesus appears to Mary as she wanders back to the tomb.

At the close of John's account of our Lord's earthly life (Jn. 21), he wrote the story of Peter's return to fishing. Peter was in a boat with the disciples. He was naked and in despair. *"Children, have you any meat?"* (Jn. 21:5) a voice called from the shoreline, unrecognized by any of them. *"Cast the net on the right side and you will find some"* (Jn. 21:6). They cast the net and the disciples were not able to bring up the multitude of fish that have been caught! John said, "It is the Lord!" Peter put on his fisher's coat and dove into the sea to meet Jesus on the shore. He arrived followed by the disciples. Jesus had prepared a fire and they ate together. Now Jesus had a plan for Peter and three times He asked, "Do you love me?" Peter responded with 'phileo', a lesser form of the word for love and a common term for brotherly love. Peter had learned not to brag. He fully understood his problem and wanted to serve his rabbi but questioned his own ability. Perhaps that is where every one of us needs to be. God's grace works in and through us.

Jesus ascended to glory, and the Father sent the Holy Spirit to His people. One hundred and twenty humble believers met in the upper room for a time of sincere prayer. Peter stood in the midst of them and began to speak, reminding the followers of the coming of the Holy Spirit.

When the day of Pentecost came, Peter stood in the midst of thousands of people – a fallen, wounded warrior empowered by the Spirit. The dispensation of the Holy Spirit came and God's Word exploded in Jerusalem. The leader was Peter. He still had his challenges and remembered his past, recognizing his new beginning. This was the man who wrote the divinely inspired Epistles of Peter. His writings, straight from God, reflect his past, present, and the firm conviction that the God he serves is the one who he cannot live without. He knows this because he was with Jesus and knew he was truly forgiven!

Now to his writings. . .

Chapter 1

WHY GOD IS GOOD
I Peter 1:1-12

"Peter, an apostle of Jesus Christ, to the pilgrims of the Dispersion in Pontus, Galatia, Cappadocia, Asia, and Bithynia, elect according to the foreknowledge of God the Father, in sanctification of the Spirit, for obedience and sprinkling of the blood of Jesus Christ: grace to you and peace be multiplied. Blessed be the God and Father of our Lord Jesus Christ, who according to His abundant mercy has begotten us again to a living hope through the resurrection of Jesus Christ from the dead, to an inheritance incorruptible and undefiled and that does not fade away, reserved in heaven for you, who are kept by the power of God through faith for salvation ready to be revealed in the last time. In this you greatly rejoice, though now for a little while, if need be, you have been grieved by various trials, that the genuineness of your faith, being much more precious than gold that perishes, though it is tested by fire, may be found to praise, honor, and glory at the revelation of Jesus Christ, whom having not seen you love. Though now you do not see Him, yet believing, you rejoice with joy inexpressible and full of glory, receiving the end of your faith—the salvation of your souls. Of this salvation the prophets have inquired and searched carefully, who prophesied of the grace that would come to you, searching what, or what manner of time, the Spirit of Christ who was in them was indicating when He testified beforehand the sufferings of Christ

and the glories that would follow. To them it was revealed that, not to themselves, but to us they were ministering the things which now have been reported to you through those who have preached the gospel to you by the Holy Spirit sent from heaven—things which angels desire to look into." **(I Pet. 1:1-12)**

*I*s God really good? This question is asked by people in every part of the world. The Apostle Peter addresses suffering in I Peter. The book commences, however, with the goodness of God.

The first 12 verses of I Peter are the doctrine of the book. The rest of it is very practical, day-by-day information to help us live the Christian life. Living out your faith for Christ produces a lens through which to view the world. It is important to have a biblical worldview for all aspects of life.

In the text, the scattered people were the diaspora (v. 1). The diaspora was a term for the Jews who lived outside of Palestine. Some of the believers that Peter addresses were also Gentile converts. Peter often writes about the salvation experience:

"As obedient children, *not conforming yourselves to the former lusts, as in your ignorance. . . knowing that you were not redeemed with corruptible things, like silver or gold, from your aimless conduct received by tradition from your father. . ."* (I Peter 1:14, 18)

"Therefore, since Christ suffered for us in the flesh, arm yourselves also with the same mind, for he who has suffered in the flesh has ceased from sin, that he no longer should live the rest of his time in the flesh for the lusts of men, but for the will of God. For we have spent enough of our past lifetime in doing the will of the Gentiles—when we walked in lewdness, lusts, drunkenness, revelries, drinking parties, and abominable idolatries. In regard to these, they think it strange that you do not run with them in the same flood of dissipation, speaking evil of you." (I Peter 4:1-4)

These Jewish and Gentile believers were scattered in five different directions. In this day Christians were disbanded because of persecution. As they traveled they evangelized; *"Therefore those who were scattered went everywhere preaching the word"* (Acts 8:4). Those scattered were not the apostles but the many converts. Bible teacher Warren Wiersbe points out in his Bible Exposition Commentary that "fifteen times in this letter, Peter referred to suffering; and he used eight different Greek words to do so." There were those who lived godly lives.

But you are a chosen generation, a royal priesthood, a holy nation, His own special people, that you may proclaim the praises of Him who called you out of darkness into His marvelous light; who once were not a people but are now the people of God, who had not obtained mercy but now have obtained mercy. Beloved, I beg you as sojourners and pilgrims, abstain from fleshly lusts which war against the soul, having your conduct honorable among the Gentiles, that when they speak against you as evildoers, they may, by your good works which they observe, glorify God in the day of visitation. Therefore submit yourselves to every ordinance of man for the Lord's sake, whether to the king as supreme, or to governors, as to those who are sent by him for the punishment of evildoers and for the praise of those who do good. For this is the will of God, that by doing good you may put to silence the ignorance of foolish men— as free, yet not using liberty as a cloak for vice, but as bondservants of God. Honor all people. Love the brotherhood. Fear God. Honor the king. Servants, be submissive to your masters with all fear, not only to the good and gentle, but also to the harsh. For this is commendable, if because of conscience toward God one endures grief, suffering wrongfully. For what credit is it if, when you are beaten for your faults, you take it patiently? But when you do good and suffer, if you take it patiently, this is commendable before God. For to this you were called, because Christ also suffered for us, leaving us an example, that you should follow His steps: "Who committed no sin, nor was deceit found in His mouth"; who, when He was reviled, did not revile in return; when He suffered, He did not threaten, but committed Himself to Him who judges righteously. . ." (I Peter 2:9-23)

"But let none of you suffer as a murderer, a thief, an evildoer, or as a busybody in other people's matters. Yet if anyone suffers as a Christian, let him not be ashamed, but let him glorify God in this matter. For the time has come for judgment to begin at the house of God; and if it begins with us first, what will be the end of those who do not obey the gospel of God? Now "If the righteous one is scarcely saved, where will the ungodly and the sinner appear?" Therefore let those who suffer according to the will of God commit their souls to Him in doing good, as to a faithful Creator." (I Peter 4:15-19)

The name of Christ exudes various responses by different people and some were reproached for the name of the Lord (I Peter 4:14).

In I Peter 4:12, the fiery trial is possibly the persecution of Christians. Jewish religionists considered Christianity a sect begun by Paul. The Roman Empire accepted Judaism but there came a day when Christianity was not considered a sect of the traditions of the Jews and the government decided to intervene. To many, Paul was "the culprit." Paul was eventually martyred after a second arrest. God provided for him a sense of calm in preparing for his death in II Tim. 4:6-8: *"For I am already being poured out as a drink offering, and the time of my departure is at hand. I have fought the good fight, I have finished the race, I have kept the faith. Finally, there is laid up for me the crown of righteousness, which the Lord, the righteous Judge, will give to me on that Day, and not to me only but also to all who have loved His appearing."*

Peter's letter becomes an encouragement. Although I do not believe the church of Jesus Christ will go through the seven years of tribulation, the fact is there may be huge persecution upon Christians prior to the return of our Lord.

The book also permeates a great lesson. This lesson is the goodness of God.

To have a biblical worldview will lead to a conclusion that God is good. The old adage that is often addressed, "God is good all the time, and all the time God is good" is true! The Bible has much to say about God's goodness. Let's go back to the very first chapter of the Bible and peruse through Scripture to see some examples of the goodness of God.

Gen. 1:10 says, *"And God called the dry land Earth; and the gathering together of the waters He called Seas. And God saw that it was good."* Verse 31 goes on to say, *"And God saw everything that he had made, and indeed it was very good."* This was after Adam had been created along with everything in the entire world. In God's eyes, all of it was good.

The fiftieth and final chapter of Genesis concludes the story of Joseph and how God was with him from slavery to the palace in Egypt. He told his brothers in verse 20, *"But as for you, you meant evil against me; but God meant it for good. . ."* Joseph knew about the goodness of God.

In Joshua 1:6, the Lord told Joshua, *"Be strong and of a good courage."* In verse 8 He gave instructions regarding His law and promised that *"you will have good success"* if those instructions were followed. Again in verse 9: *"Be strong and of a good courage."*

Near the end of his life, Joshua gave his farewell address in chapter 23. By this time the children of Israel had arrived in the Promised Land. The arrival pictures the victorious Christian life. It is the good life.

In verse 13 Joshua refers to *"this good land which the Lord your God has given you."* In verse 14 he mentions *"all the good things which the Lord your God spoke concerning you."*

Look at verses 15-16. *"Therefore it shall come to pass, that as all the good things have come upon you which the Lord your God promised you, so the Lord will bring upon you all harmful things, until He has destroyed you from this good land which the Lord your God has given you. When you have transgressed the covenant of the Lord your God, which He commanded you, and have gone and served other gods, and bowed down to them, then the anger of the Lord will burn against you, and you shall perish quickly from the good land which He has given you."* Joshua repeatedly used the word "good" to describe their situation. I like to call Joshua 23 "How to live the good life."

We can find more of this in the Psalms. We all know the words of Ps. 23:6. *"Surely goodness and mercy shall follow me all the days of my life: and I will dwell in the house of the Lord forever."* Psalm 73 begins with these words: *"Truly God is good to Israel."*

The rich young ruler who came to Jesus in Mt. 19:16 said, *"Good Teacher, what good thing shall I do that I may have eternal life?"* Christ's response in verse 17: *"Why do you call Me good? No one is good but One, that is, God."* We have a good God.

The Apostle Paul emphasizes this point in Rom. 2:4. *"Or do you despise the riches of His goodness, forbearance, and longsuffering, not knowing that the goodness of God leads you to repentance?"*

James 1:17 says, *"Every good gift and every perfect gift is from above."* I submit to you that from all of these verses we can conclude that God is good all the time.

The word *good* can be translated as favor. God is good. He wants us to have a favored life. Let's look now at chapter 1 of I Peter and note what He has provided. In the first two verses of I Peter 1, we see that it is because of the family He has provided. The people reading this book represent a large number of different churches. There are likely various nationalities and people from many different states, different political affiliations, married and single people, and so on. We have so many differences, but there is one thing that draws us together and that is our Lord and Savior, Jesus Christ.

Again, look at verses 1-2. *"Peter, an apostle of Jesus Christ, to the pilgrims of the Dispersion in Pontus, Galatia, Cappadocia, Asia, and Bithynia, elect according to the foreknowledge of God the Father, in sanctification of the Spirit, for obedience and sprinkling of the blood of Jesus Christ: grace to you and peace be multiplied."*

Peter was one of the original 12 disciples of Christ. He likely wrote this epistle around 60 A.D. and we can surmise from chapter 5 that at least part of it was written in Babylon. Peter was an interesting man.

It is important to remember that we should not let ourselves get too attached to this world. If you ask me where I live, as of this writing I live near Binghamton, New York where I have lived much of my life. I lived for 25 years in Chambersburg, Pennsylvania where I was pastor of a church. Another 14 years I lived in the Miami/Fort Lauderdale area where I served as a pastor. "Home" means different things to different people depending on when they are talking about it. But as Christians, our home is in Heaven.

The people depicted as "scattered" in verse 1 are also described this way in verse 2: ". . . *elect according to the foreknowledge of God the Father, in sanctification of the Spirit, for obedience and sprinkling of the blood of Jesus Christ: grace to you and peace be multiplied.*"

The word *foreknowledge* is the word from which we get "prognosis." It shows that God knew to take us in the wretched, sinful condition that we were in. It means that God set His love on us in a personal way. God set His love on Israel; He chose them. The Father chose us, the Son redeemed us and the Holy Spirit has set us apart from the unbelievers.

To be sanctified means to be set apart, which is what happens to people at salvation and continues throughout the Christian life. God's people are set apart for God.

There are three tenses used to describe sanctification. The first is **past** tense. We were saved out of sin and separated unto Jesus Christ. **Present** tense means that God has saved us and we belong to Him alone. **Future** sanctification is that one day, we will have a body that is glorious.

Peter is writing these words to heartbroken people who have been dispersed and are going through a difficult time. He greets and salutes them as fellow Christians who are in the same family – the family of God. How wonderful to be a part of that family.

If you are traveling somewhere in the world and feeling alone, you may walk into a church and find people with whom you connect. It is a unique feeling. There is nothing like being in the family of God.

The sanctifying work is done through the work of the Holy Spirit. The term "for obedience and sprinkling of the blood of Jesus Christ" is the work of the Son. The work of the Spirit is to set aside His people and the Father chose us before the foundation of the world. The Son of God saved me through His blood on the cross and the Holy Spirit convicts and regenerates the sinner. " *And I will pray the Father, and He will give you another Helper, that He may abide with you forever"* (John 14:14-16). Believers make a decision. I Peter 1:23 states *". . . having been born again, not of corruptible seed but incorruptible, through the word of God which lives and abides forever. . ."*

In verses 3-9 God's goodness is seen by the abundance He provides. Verse 3 says, *"Blessed be the God and Father of our Lord Jesus Christ, who according to His abundant mercy has begotten us again to a living hope through the resurrection of Jesus Christ from the dead. . ."*

You and I have mercy through the resurrection of Jesus Christ. That resurrection is the linchpin of our Christian faith and the keystone of all teaching.

For years I have taken groups of people to the Holy Land. One of the highlights of that trip is a visit to the empty tomb. There are two traditional locations. One is the Church of the Holy Sepulchre, the other is named The Garden Tomb. Because of its ambiance, I prefer the latter. The Garden Tomb was discovered by British Major-General Charles George Gordon when he was staying in the apartment of Horatio Spafford, who is known for writing the beloved gospel song *It Is Well With My Soul.* I personally enjoy the Garden Tomb. We go up the hill and view Golgotha where we usually hear a brilliant British lecturer talk about the crucifixion and resurrection of Christ. After we pass the cistern, everyone has the opportunity to walk in and out of the empty tomb.

Many times I have seen people walk out of that tomb weeping. It is an emotional experience. People spend thousands of dollars to go halfway around the world and see a tomb that contains nothing. Aren't you glad that no one is in that grave today?

It is amusing to me that every year around Easter there is a new theory about what happened to Jesus Christ. Most of these theories try to avoid the fact that Jesus rose from the grave. One day those "experts" will stop theorizing, because *"at the name of Jesus every knee should bow, of things in heaven, and things in earth, and things under the earth; And that every tongue should confess that Jesus Christ is Lord, to the glory of God the Father"* (Phil. 2:10-11).

The word hope in both Old and New Testaments is best defined as confidence. Hope is in the future as it states in Romans 8:23-24, *"Not only that, but we also who have the firstfruits of the Spirit, even we ourselves groan within ourselves, eagerly waiting for the adoption, the redemption of our body. For we were saved in this hope, but hope that is seen is not hope; for why does one still hope for what he sees?"* This scripture teaches that if you have something or see it then it is no longer hope. 1 Peter 1: 4 calls this hope an inheritance. Note that this inheritance cannot be ruined – incorruptible. It cannot be insignificant or changed in any way – undefiled. It is forever – eternal. We are included in Christ's last will and testament. *". . . Who are kept by the power of God through faith for salvation ready to be revealed in the last time. . . receiving the end of your faith—the salvation of your souls"* (I Peter 1:5, 9). This inheritance refers to our salvation. It also refers to the coming of Jesus! One day we will have new bodies! We one day will have the body that God intended for us. It is a glorious body and God's glory is and will be forever. Amazingly He desires to share this glory with us. Glory refers to the totality, if that is possible, of God! Glory is the sum total of God's love, holiness, faithfulness, immutability, or any other characteristic we can mention.

Many years ago when my parents were alive, they had some wealthy friends who put them in their will. After my father died that will was changed to include my wife and me.

Unbeknownst to us, some other relatives were taking the possessions of the surviving lady while she was alive. After she died I went to see the attorney and he said, "I'm sorry to tell you that the only things left for you are a green chair and two diamond rings." I thought the rings might be valuable, but a jeweler told me that both of them added up to about $66 in value. They weren't diamond rings after all.

I thought about this entire situation and pondered how earthly wealth can disappear so easily. On the other hand, we as Christians have an inheritance that will never pass away and is kept by none other than Almighty God.

This takes us to verse 5. *"Who are kept by the power of God through faith unto salvation ready to be revealed in the last time."*

The word *kept* in that verse is a military term meaning to be guarded or protected. That is how strongly God keeps and protects us in times of trial and heartache. Here is the essence of the goodness of God. We are kept for God's glory. We are protected, prepared, and promoted for this glory. Now here is the apex for us: we have already been glorified as we see in Romans 8:30, *"Moreover whom He predestined, these He also called; whom He called, these He also justified; and whom He justified, these He also glorified."* The only thing that remains is God's publically portraying it for us in glory! Nothing in this life fully satisfies! When we are with Him one day, we will understand. God made us for this! To be with Him!

The next few verses are the key to the entire book of I Peter as they answer the question we asked earlier about why good people seem to have such awful things happen in their lives.

Look at verses 6-7. *"In this you greatly rejoice, though now for a little while, if need be, you have been grieved by various trials, that the genuineness of your faith, being much more precious than gold that perishes, though it is tested by fire, may be found to praise, honor, and glory at the revelation of Jesus Christ."* That opening phrase is also translated as *"the trial of your faith."* We are here for the glory of God.

It is easy to say that we have real faith, but we only know what kind of faith we have when it is tested by fire, similar to testing gold. When gold is refined by fire it becomes more valuable as its purity is better determined. In the same manner, troubles and trials test and refine us for the glory of God. The fact is we are already fully prepared for glorification. We are kept for God's glory.

Bible commentator, Alfred Sorenson put it well when he said, "Throughout the Bible, people whom God greatly uses were always tested first." None of us like to be tested. Testing either draws us to the Lord or drives us away from Him. It can make you better or bitter.

In verse 6, Peter uses the term *manifold* to describe the temptations. It is an artistic term which means "many colors". There are many different types of trials. They can lead to depression and discouragement. Trials are painful. They are not to be taken lightly. Thankfully, they only last for a period of time and then pass over (for a season). Gold goes through the smelting furnace in order that it may "look" gold! As we go through suffering the goal is to make us reflect on our Lord and Savior Jesus Christ (Job 23:10).

His mercy becomes a teacher, as seen in verses 8-9. *"Whom having not seen, ye love; in whom, though now ye see him not, yet believing, ye rejoice with joy unspeakable and full of glory: Receiving the end of your faith, even the salvation of your souls."*

When you go through life's trials you see God strengthening, encouraging and helping you. He is working even when others cannot see or understand it.

The great writers of God in the Old Testament did not understand these next two verses and the angels of God to this day do not understand it. As we see in verses 10-12, the goodness of God is seen in His amazing grace.

"Of which salvation the prophets have enquired and searched diligently, who prophesied of the grace that should come unto you: Searching what, or what manner of time the Spirit of Christ which was in them did signify, when it testified beforehand the sufferings of Christ, and the glory that should follow. Unto whom it was revealed, that not unto themselves, but unto us they did minister the things, which are now reported unto you by them that have preached the gospel unto you with the Holy Ghost sent down from heaven; which things the angels desire to look into."

A very familiar verse during the Christmas season is Isaiah 9:6, *"For unto us a child is born, unto us a son is given: and the government shall be upon his shoulder: and his name shall be called Wonderful, Counsellor, The mighty God, The everlasting Father, The Prince of Peace."* This verse describes the first time He came to the earth. This was the Incarnation. God the Son came to the earth as a man.

Now look at the next verse, Isaiah 9:7, *"Of the increase of his government and peace there shall be no end, upon the throne of David, and upon his kingdom, to order it, and to establish it with judgment and with justice from henceforth even for ever. The zeal of the LORD of hosts will perform this."* This illustrates His triumphant return as King of Kings and Lord of Lords. The prophets of old did not understand the timing between the Son of God's first coming and His second coming back to the earth. They seemed to understand that it was all one event.

Based on their knowledge of the Old Testament, the disciples often asked Jesus when He would set up His kingdom. The writers of the Old Testament did not fully understand the death, burial and resurrection of Christ. Once they lived through those events with Jesus, the disciples knew the events of Christ's death and resurrection.

The book of I Peter takes a turn beginning in verse 13, as we begin to learn that our motivation to live for the Lord is the privileged position we have in Jesus Christ. The first 12 verses show us what God has done for us, while the remainder of the epistle talks about our influence in other people's lives.

The apostle now begins to emphasize our day to day walk or conduct. We are looking for Jesus to come again. For the believer, we will either see Christ's return or meet Him upon death. This is the believers hope. Hope is not wishing, it is the confident expectation of seeing our Lord Jesus Christ.

I was amazed at how God allows us to influence other people's lives when we least expect it. As we go through trials and God refines us like gold, He allows others to see what is happening to us and it serves as a challenge to them.

Our God is a very good God. He is good all the time and all the time God is good. He is continually working with us so that we will be what He wants us to be, here in this world and until that day we will be with Him forever.

Questions:
1. What does diaspora mean?
2. What is one of the meanings of *good?*
3. We have mercy through the linchpin of the Christian faith. What is the linchpin?
4. The word *kept* is a military term meaning to be _____ or _____ .

Discussion:
1. What experiences have you gone through that have refined your life?

Chapter 2

THE LORD IS COMING
I Peter 1:13

"Wherefore gird up the loins of your mind, be sober, and hope to the end for the grace that is to be brought unto you at the revelation of Jesus Christ. . ." **(I Peter 1:13)**

*W*e all have moments in history that we will never forget. Depending upon your age, it could be the attack on Pearl Harbor or the assassination of President Kennedy. Those events cause us to stop and remember exactly where you were and when you heard about it. In 2001 another event of that magnitude gripped the hearts of a new generation of Americans. It is the now famous 9/11.

I attended the American Association of Christian Schools convention in Washington, D.C. About 70 pastors and educators in our group were going to the White House for a briefing. It was a beautiful day. As the bus made its way there that morning, the leader of our tour group mentioned that a plane had just hit the World Trade Center. Most of us did not think much about it, imagining that a small plane had struck that huge building and killed a small number of people.

We got off the bus and were about to walk into a side entrance of the White House – I was only a few feet from the door – when a woman came running out crying and yelling. I wondered what had happened to her, but the next moment a guard came outside and said, "There is a plane coming full-throttle to the White House. Run to J Street!"

I did not know where J Street was located, but I knew what it meant to run. I led the pack. I found out later that there was no J Street and the guard had actually said "G Street," but we raced away from the White House nonetheless.

Out on the street, a woman cried, "My husband is back there!" I tried to calm her, telling her that this event couldn't possibly be that serious and everyone would be fine. Then someone told us that the plane which was coming toward the White House had swerved and hit the Pentagon. We all looked in the direction of the Pentagon and saw a giant cloud of smoke in the distance.

What had begun as a very quiet day in Washington became a day of absolute chaos. We all had to walk back to our hotel (I had to ask where it was). I tried to call my wife and could not get through because the cell phone lines were overwhelmed. My daughter called me later in tears because she wanted to know if I was all right.

We reached the hotel and there was already a great deal of added security. We were told we would have to give a picture ID again to make certain we were actually staying there. When I arrived in my room I turned on the television and finally saw the images of the World Trade Center just after being attacked. If you asked me what I felt when I saw it, the best way I could describe would be that it was surreal. I could not believe it was happening.

There is a theme that runs constantly through the book of I Peter regarding the goodness of God as well as an event that we should all be ready for. In fact, I and II Peter lead up to this cataclysmic event.

Verse 13 of chapter 1 says, "*Wherefore gird up the loins of your mind, be sober, and hope to the end for the grace that is to be brought unto you at the revelation of Jesus Christ.*"

The word "*revelation*" in this verse means the unveiling of Jesus Christ. An underlying theme in I Peter is this unveiling, which may seem surreal to many people but should not be to Christians. We should be expecting it. We need to think about this one verse and it's depth of meaning.

Go back to verses 3-5 for a moment. *"Blessed be the God and Father of our Lord Jesus Christ, which according to his abundant mercy hath begotten us again unto a lively hope by the resurrection of Jesus Christ from the dead, To an inheritance incorruptible, and undefiled, and that fadeth not away, reserved in heaven for you, Who are kept by the power of God through faith unto salvation ready to be revealed in the last time."*

That *"lively hope"* is also referred to in scripture as a *"blessed hope."* It speaks not just of what we have now but what is to come. The final part of that passage refers to something that will be *"revealed,"* similar to the unveiling we just saw in verse 13.

We discussed in the previous chapter that our true home is in Heaven. This fact is reinforced in I Pet. 2:11, which begins, *"Dearly beloved, I beseech you as strangers and pilgrims."*

Peter makes a reference to suffering, which we will look at more closely later, as well as another cataclysmic event we are all familiar with. I Pet. 3:20 says, *"Which sometime were disobedient, when once the longsuffering of God waited in the days of Noah, while the ark was a preparing, wherein few, that is, eight souls were saved by water."* God uses the Flood here as a reminder of the need for long-suffering during such a trying time.

Soon after that, I Pet. 4:7 give a warning about another cataclysmic event. *"But the end of all things is at hand: be ye therefore sober, and watch unto prayer."* This verse makes it clear that Christians should be expecting the Lord's return and, in fact, be preparing for it.

In the first chapter of II Peter, the apostle is talking about his own demise and predicting that he will soon die, but he also addresses the future of the Kingdom and Christ's coming. II Pet. 1:16 says, *"For we have not followed cunningly devised fables, when we made known unto you the power and coming of our Lord Jesus Christ, but were eyewitnesses of his majesty."* This is a reference to the fact that Peter was present for such events as Christ's transfiguration and heard God the Father say, *"This is my beloved Son, in whom I am well pleased"* (Matt. 17:5). Jesus pleased the Father while on the earth, and we are to please the Father as well. Part of what pleases Him is our expectancy of the Lord's impending return.

The longer we live here, the more acutely aware we are that fewer and fewer people are talking about the coming of the Lord. The first three verses of II Peter 2 talk about destructive doctrines in the last days.

"But there were false prophets also among the people, even as there shall be false teachers among you, who privily shall bring in damnable heresies, even denying the Lord that bought them, and bring upon themselves swift destruction. And many shall follow their pernicious ways; by reason of whom the way of truth shall be evil spoken of. And through covetousness shall they with feigned words make merchandise of you: whose judgment now of a long time lingereth not, and their damnation slumbereth not."

There are churches today that used to preach the gospel but no longer do. Every church that claims to be Christian should have at the heart of its message the gospel of Jesus Christ – His death, burial and resurrection.

Verses 4-11 talk about false prophets. In these verses we are reminded that God judged nations in the past, and we should not expect anything less today.

"For if God spared not the angels that sinned, but cast them down to hell, and delivered them into chains of darkness, to be reserved unto judgment; And spared not the old world, but saved Noah the eighth person, a preacher of righteousness, bringing in the flood upon the world of the ungodly; And turning the cities of Sodom and Gomorrha into ashes condemned them with an over-throw, making them an ensample unto those that after should live ungodly; And delivered just Lot, vexed with the filthy conversation of the wicked: (For that righteous man dwelling among them, in seeing and hearing, vexed his righteous soul from day to day with their unlawful deeds;) The Lord knoweth how to deliver the godly out of temptations, and to reserve the unjust unto the day of judgment to be punished: But chiefly them that walk after the flesh in the lust of uncleanness, and despise government. Presumptuous are they, self-willed, they are not afraid to speak evil of dignities. Whereas angels, which are greater in power and might, bring not railing accusation against them before the Lord."

The main topic of verses 12-17 is the depravity of false teachers. There are many in the ministry for reasons other than the sake of the gospel, and this passage gives many illustrations about these kinds of people.

"But these, as natural brute beasts, made to be taken and destroyed, speak evil of the things that they understand not; and shall utterly perish in their own corruption; And shall receive the reward of unrighteousness, as they that count it pleasure to riot in the day time. Spots they are and blemishes, sporting themselves with their own deceivings while they feast with you; Having eyes full of adultery, and that cannot cease from sin; beguiling unstable souls: an heart they have exercised with covetous practices; cursed children: Which have forsaken the right way, and are gone astray, following the way of Balaam the son of Bosor, who loved the wages of unrighteousness; But was rebuked for his iniquity: the dumb ass speaking with man's voice forbad the madness of the prophet. These are wells without water, clouds that are carried with a tempest; to whom the mist of darkness is reserved for ever."

I am president of a college and I understand very well how it needs money to operate, but if I make money the main focus of my ministry I will sink to the same kind of depravity that is described here. One of the biggest sins in my own country in recent decades has been its emphasis on materialism and the covetousness that has developed as a result.

The second chapter of II Peter concludes with a discussion of the deception of false teachers in verses 18-22. *"For when they speak great swelling words of vanity, they allure through the lusts of the flesh, through much wantonness, those that were clean escaped from them who live in error. While they promise them liberty, they themselves are the servants of corruption: for of whom a man is overcome, of the same is he brought in bondage. For if after they have escaped the pollutions of the world through the knowledge of the Lord and Saviour Jesus Christ, they are again entangled therein, and overcome, the latter end is worse with them than the beginning. For it had been better for them not to have known the way of righteousness, than, after they have known it, to turn from the holy commandment delivered unto them. But it is happened unto them according to the true proverb, The dog is turned to his own vomit again; and the sow that was washed to her wallowing in the mire."*

We have to be very careful about some things in the society in which we now live. For instance, you will often hear politicians and government leader's talk about "freedom of worship," which sounds very good. Many times, however, the intent of that phrase is to suggest that we worship within the walls of our own churches and not take it outside those walls. What we actually have (and what we want) is freedom of religion, and we need to study the Word of God in our churches but also take it out and share it with those in the world around us.

Another popular concept today is the idea that salvation is possible through some means other than the Lord Jesus Christ. We know that is not true, and we should challenge those who think otherwise with this: Who else rose from the grave? What other religion has a risen savior?

A dangerous idea that goes hand in hand with this is the philosophy that all truth is subjective – you have your truth, I have mine, let's just believe what we want to believe and we'll all live happily ever after. We are in the post modern era. All of these ideas are representative of what is addressed here in II Peter 2 and we should see them as confirmation that the return of our Lord is imminent.

It is interesting that many Christians do not think about the coming of Christ except when we are specifically challenged to do so. We need to be reminded of what awaits us beyond this life. Let's look at II Pet. 3:1-3 with this thought in mind.

"This second epistle, beloved, I now write unto you; in both which I stir up your pure minds by way of remembrance: That ye may be mindful of the words which were spoken before by the holy prophets, and of the commandment of us the apostles of the Lord and Saviour: Knowing this first, that there shall come in the last days scoffers, walking after their own lusts."

It is amusing to see how many people can read a book of science fiction or watch a popular movie and think that it could really happen, but if you were to suggest that the Lord will soon return they look at you like you are crazy.

The word *"scoffers"* in this passage reflect back to New Testament times to those who openly questioned the very existence of God. Note these verses:

Mal. 2:17, *"Ye have wearied the LORD with your words. Yet ye say, wherein have we wearied him? When ye say, every one that doeth evil is good in the sight of the LORD, and he delighteth in them; or, where is the God of judgment?"*

Ps. 42:3, *"My tears have been my meat day and night, while they continually say unto me, where is thy God?"*

Ps. 79:10, *"Wherefore should the heathen say, where is their God? Let him be known among the heathen in our sight by the revenging of the blood of thy servants which is shed."*

Jer. 17:15, *"Behold, they say unto me, where is the word of the LORD? Let it come now."*

When a scoffer asks about the whereabouts of God, he is actually stating that he does not believe God exists. Peter gives their explanation in II Peter 3.

Look at verse 4, *"And saying, where is the promise of his coming? For since the fathers fell asleep, all things continue as they were from the beginning of the creation."* They say that since nothing has happened over the thousands of years since creation, and so many generations have come and gone, there is no reason to expect Christ to come now.

He refutes this argument in verse 5-7. *"For this they willingly are ignorant of, that by the word of God the heavens were of old, and the earth standing out of the water and in the water: Whereby the world that then was, being overflowed with water, perished: But the heavens and the earth, which are now, by the same word are kept in store, reserved unto fire against the day of judgment and perdition of ungodly men."*

The fire mentioned in this passage is not an isolated reference. There are many such references in the Bible. According to Ps. 50:3, *"Our God shall come, and shall not keep silence: a fire shall devour before him, and it shall be very tempestuous round about him."*

Isa. 29:6 says, *"Thou shalt be visited of the LORD of hosts with thunder, and with earthquake, and great noise, with storm and tempest, and the flame of devouring fire."*

Look at Isa. 30:30. *"And the LORD shall cause his glorious voice to be heard, and shall shew the lighting down of his arm, with the indignation of his anger, and with the flame of a devouring fire, with scattering, and tempest, and hailstones."*

Here are the words of Malachi 4:1. *"For, behold, the day cometh, that shall burn as an oven; and all the proud, yea, and all that do wickedly, shall be stubble: and the day that cometh shall burn them up, saith the LORD of hosts, that it shall leave them neither root nor branch."*

These are just a few of the many verses in the Bible that speak about fire. Many geologists today claim that there is a sort of internal combustion within the earth itself – a fire burning within. With that in mind, it is especially noteworthy that Peter mentions the use of fire as an instrument of judgment.

Our material possessions will one day go up in smoke. None of it will last. I think about the home my wife and I purchased when we moved to Davis College in upstate New York. It is a beautiful house on a wonderful piece of land and we want to enjoy it for many years, but it will be gone one day. All of the things we enjoy in this life will eventually be gone.

As for those who continue to ask why the Lord has not come, II Peter 3:8 provides this reminder: *"But, beloved, be not ignorant of this one thing, that one day is with the Lord as a thousand years, and a thousand years as one day."*

I made the mistake once of telling one of my grandchildren that someone would be coming to our house in two weeks. Several times that day, she asked me, "Are they here yet?" As every parent knows, very young children have little or no concept of time as we look at it. Likewise, our concept of time is totally different from the way God looks at it. God always considers history in light of the eternal present.

I am now at the age where I would love to see Jesus Christ come again. When I was young and in love with my future wife, however, I did not want him to come before I was married. It was the same when my children came along, as I wanted to see them grow up. We all think about these things, but God does not consider time in this way at all. Ps. 90:4 says, *"For a thousand years in thy sight are but as yesterday when it is past, and as a watch in the night."*

When we remember His attitude toward time, we should consider that every single day is certainly a gift from God.

As for the prevailing attitude in Peter's time about the Lord having not returned, II Pet. 3:9 gives a good reason for the perceived delay. *"The Lord is not slack concerning his promise, as some men count slackness; but is longsuffering to us-ward, not willing that any should perish, but that all should come to repentance."* God is not tardy. He is always on time.

I know we all believe what that verse says, but we do not always live like it. We all have family members and friends who need Christ. The Bible tells us that there will come a day when the last soul is brought into the family of God, and when that happens our Lord will come again. That time has not come yet, and the Lord wants everyone to have the opportunity the come to Him.

One of our students at Davis College recently preached his first sermon on a Sunday night and someone was saved at the service. A few days later I asked him how the service went and he said, "I understand now why pastors often take Monday off. I was exhausted at the end of the service. I put everything I had into it, but it was worth it because a soul was saved." I saw tears in his eyes as he told me this.

That is the bottom line. The main goal of everything we do should be to see people come to Christ and to grow in the Christian faith. I am so glad I had parents who loved me enough to tell me about Jesus. My father had been unsaved for many years, but when he accepted Christ (my mother was already saved) he thought we should go to church and we went every time the doors were opened. I was a young boy at the time, and I didn't really want to go to church. There were plenty of things I would rather be doing.

One summer I went to Vacation Bible School and when I got home the first day, my mother asked if I liked it. "No," I said.

"Do you want to go back tomorrow?"

"No."

"Then you don't have to."

I was thrilled until I heard the next words out of her mouth. "We're going to have Bible school right here at home."

Suddenly I wanted to go back to VBS but it was too late. She took me out on the back porch of our home and opened her Bible to the book of Isaiah. I didn't know a lot about the Bible at that time but I knew Isaiah was a big book. I wondered if she was going to cover the entire book right there with me.

She found Isaiah 2:10 and read it to me. *"Enter into the rock, and hide thee in the dust, for fear of the LORD, and for the glory of his majesty."* I have never heard of anyone before or since who accepted Christ based upon that verse, but she led me to Jesus right there.

"Son, the reason you don't want to go to church is because you're a sinner," she said. "You're lost."

Once I accepted Christ I liked going to church. I went back to VBS and liked it. Something had changed. God wants everyone to have the chance at salvation.

We find in II Peter 3:10 the surreal event I alluded to when talking about the 9/11 attacks or the JFK assassination. *"But the day of the Lord will come as a thief in the night; in which the heavens shall pass away with a great noise, and the elements shall melt with fervent heat, the earth also and the works that are therein shall be burned up."*

The phrase *"the day of the Lord"* refers not to a single event but a period of time beginning with the rapture. Coming *"as a thief in the night"* means that God is not going to announce the time of His coming in advance.

Isaiah 13:9 says, *"Behold, the day of the LORD cometh, cruel both with wrath and fierce anger, to lay the land desolate: and he shall destroy the sinners thereof out of it."*

Look at Zephaniah 1:14. *"The great day of the LORD is near, it is near, and hasteth greatly, even the voice of the day of the LORD: the mighty man shall cry there bitterly. That day is a day of wrath, a day of trouble and distress, a day of wasteness and desolation, a day of darkness and gloominess, a day of clouds and thick darkness."*

These verses describe events that will change our world in an extraordinary way.

With all of this in mind, consider the challenge in I Pet. 3:11-13. *"Seeing then that all these things shall be dissolved, what manner of persons ought ye to be in all holy conversation and godliness, Looking for and hasting unto the coming of the day of God, wherein the heavens being on fire shall be dissolved, and the elements shall melt with fervent heat? Nevertheless we, according to his promise, look for new heavens and a new earth, wherein dwelleth righteousness."*

That promise from God at the end of verse 13 is so important to us. We have all experienced the disappointment in someone's broken promise, but we know that God's promises will never be broken. Christ came once, and He will certainly come again.

Now go back to I Peter 1:13. *"Wherefore gird up the loins of your mind, be sober, and hope to the end for the grace that is to be brought unto you at the revelation of Jesus Christ."* Having seen some of the verses that follow this passage, we can understand better that *"revelation"* Peter is talking about here. God is good all the time – so good that He wants to remind us how He will come back someday and take us to be with Him.

Knowing all of this, we also have a plan provided by God for dealing with this news about the end times. According to II Peter 3:14-16, *"Wherefore, beloved, seeing that ye look for such things, be diligent that ye may be found of him in peace, without spot, and blameless. And account that the longsuffering of our Lord is salvation; even as our beloved brother Paul also according to the wisdom given unto him hath written unto you; As also in all his epistles, speaking in them of these things; in which are some things hard to be understood, which they that are unlearned and unstable wrest, as they do also the other scriptures, unto their own destruction."*

As we get closer to the coming of Christ, the scriptures will be twisted in many different directions. We are warned in verses 17-18 not to become a victim of this practice. *"Ye therefore, beloved, seeing ye know these things before, beware lest ye also, being led away with the error of the wicked, fall from your own steadfastness. But grow in grace, and in the knowledge of our Lord and Savior Jesus Christ. To him be glory both now and forever. Amen."*

There is nothing better than knowing and understanding the Word of God. As we increase in our knowledge of the Bible, it drives us to the ultimate truth that Jesus is everything.

I heard a story about a man who held an auction to sell many of his possessions. One of the items he presented was a picture of his only son who had died years before, but no one wanted to bid on it. Someone shouted that he wanted to move on and bid on the valuables in the sale, but the man insisted on auctioning the picture. It was finally sold for one dollar.

"The auction is now over," the man announced to the stunned crowd. "The person who purchased the picture of my son receives the rest of my inheritance."

Whoever has received the Son of God also gets the inheritance of our Lord. When you have Jesus, you have everything.

I was a pastor for 25 years in Pennsylvania and had the privilege of leading some wonderful people. One of them was a man named Stu Snyder who was in his eighties when he said to me, "I will not die until Jesus comes."

Months later I received a phone call that Stu was in the hospital. I went to the hospital to see him. Stu was the kind of person who told you whatever happened to be on his mind at any particular time.

"Did you see them?" he asked me as I arrived.

"Who?" I asked.

"You know."

"No, I don't."

We went back and forth for a minute and I thought he was delirious. I stepped outside to speak with the medical staff and they told me, "We lost him for a moment and he came back."

I went back in and asked Stu, "Do you think you saw the angels of God?"

He pointed his finger at me and said, "I told you, you knew, what I was talking about."

I reminded him about his prediction that he would live to see the Lord return and he said, "I'm going to be with the Lord today."

"No, you're not."

"Yes, I am."

This went on for a while as well. Finally I prayed with him and left. When I arrived home I received a phone call informing me that my dear friend had gone home to be with the Lord. I thought about what a wonderful moment it must have been, *"to be absent from the body, and to be present with the Lord"* (II Cor. 5:8).

The late T.E. Koshy, who was one of our Board members at the college I oversee, shared with me about a man born into a Sikh family who grew up to hate Christianity. As a young man he took a stack of copies of the gospel of John and burned them in front of his friends. Three days later he was converted and he became known as a wandering preacher in certain parts of India.

One day he visited a Hindu college and as he spoke, a lecturer came after him aggressively and began to rebuke him. "What did you ever find in Christianity that you did not find in other religions?" he asked.

"I found Christ," the man replied.

"But what was the doctrine, the principle, the teaching, that moved you?" the man asked.

"You don't understand," the preacher replied. "It was Jesus."

That is what it's all about. It is Jesus and nothing else.

Let me give you three thoughts about the coming of the Lord.

Always look up. Expect Jesus to come. We will be rewarded for that.

Look out. Seek people who need the Lord. We have a responsibility to tell them.

Live on. Enjoy your life knowing what great things you have to look forward to.

Robert Sumner was an evangelist. He was preaching in a meeting about the coming of the Lord, and many people brought friends to hear him. One woman brought her husband but he was unaffected by the message.

On the ride home that night, their son in the back seat was thinking about the fact that people could be left behind when Jesus comes. He asked his mother, "If Jesus comes, will my Dad be left behind?"

Fearful that her husband was listening and would not come back to church, the woman told her son not to talk about this subject in the car. They went home and the boy was put to bed, but they heard him come back down the steps. He had tears in his eyes.

"Mom, will Dad be left behind?" he asked again.

The boy's father could not sleep that night or concentrate on his work the next day. Finally he told his wife, "I don't want my son worried about his daddy being left behind." He bowed his head in the living room and trusted Christ as his Savior.

The Lord could return today, or it could be years from now. We should live our lives with this in mind, knowing that we please the Father when we follow the Son.

Questions:
1. The 'lively hope' is also referred to us as the _____ .
2. Every church that claims to be Christian should have what at the heart of their message?
3. What is the meaning of the word 'revelation'?

Discussion:
1. Since Jesus is coming, how should we live?

Chapter 3

LIVING A CLEAN LIFE
I Peter 1:14-25

"As obedient children, not fashioning yourselves according to the former lusts in your ignorance: but as he which hath called you is holy, so be ye holy in all manner of conversation; because it is written, Be ye holy; for I am holy. And if ye call on the Father, who without respect of persons judgeth according to every man's work, pass the time of your sojourning here in fear: forasmuch as ye know that ye were not redeemed with corruptible things, as silver and gold, from your vain conversation received by tradition from your fathers; but with the precious blood of Christ, as of a lamb without blemish and without spot: who verily was foreordained before the foundation of the world, but was manifest in these last times for you, who by him do believe in God, that raised him up from the dead, and gave him glory; that your faith and hope might be in God. Seeing ye have purified your souls in obeying the truth through the Spirit unto unfeigned love of the brethren, see that ye love one another with a pure heart fervently: being born again, not of corruptible seed, but of incorruptible, by the word of God, which liveth and abideth for ever. For all flesh is as grass, and all the glory of man as the flower of grass. The grass withereth, and the flower thereof falleth away: but the word of the Lord endureth for ever. And this is the word which by the gospel is preached unto you." **(I Peter 1:14-25)**

O bedience is the outgrowth of a changed life. Prior to our salvation we were "ignorant" of true obedience to Christ. Often people claim to accept Christ to improve their marriage, have a better life, or to be better parents. Others face a crisis and want God when they are going through heartache. Although God may use events to bring us to Christ, there is only one reason to be saved. The only reason someone needs Christ is because we are a sinner in need of a Savior. God's grace is His wonderful provision. I am not sure who originally said it, but using an acrostic, grace is God's riches at Christ's expense! Ephesians 2:1-3 declares, *"And you hath he quickened, who were dead in trespasses and sins; wherein in time past ye walked according to the course of this world, according to the prince of the power of the air, the spirit that now worketh in the children of disobedience: among whom also we all had our conversation in times past in the lusts of our flesh, fulfilling the desires of the flesh and of the mind; and were by nature the children of wrath, even as others."* But in Ephesians 1:4, God reminds Christ's followers of His abundant mercy and grace. When one comes to Christ change is inevitable!

The word *"holy"* means set apart or different. It is wonderful to have grace and to allow God to direct our lives but to live a holy life is a challenge. The world is full of temptation and sin. In verse 15, God has called us to a holy life! *"For I am the Lord your God: ye shall therefore sanctify yourselves, and ye shall be holy; for I am holy: neither shall ye defile yourselves with any manner of creeping thing that creepeth upon the earth. For I am the Lord that bringeth you up out of the land of Egypt, to be your God: ye shall therefore be holy, for I am holy"* (Leviticus 11:44-45). No one can live this life apart from Jesus Christ.

The key to learning this life is the Word of God. In his remarkable worldwide evangelistic ministry, Billy Graham would often thunder "The Bible says . . ." The same is true for our walk and obedience to Christ. The issue is, "What does the Bible say?" I need to learn obedience. There are times when we need comfort. There are hundreds of precious promises like the familiar words of Psalms 23:1-6, *"The Lord is my shepherd; I shall not want. He makes me to lie down in green pastures: he leadeth me beside the still waters. He restoreth my soul: he leadeth me in the paths of righteousness for his name's sake. Yea, though I walk through the valley of the shadow of death, I will fear no evil: for thou art with me; thy rod and thy staff they comfort me. Thou preparest a table before me in the presence of mine enemies: thou anointest my head with oil; my cup runneth over. Surely goodness and mercy shall follow me all the days of my life: and I will dwell in the house of the Lord forever."*

There are occasions when we are in a battle and we need strength. Passages like Ephesians 6:10-17 help. *"Finally, my brethren, be strong in the Lord, and in the power of his might. Put on the whole armour of God, that ye may be able to stand against the wiles of the devil. For we wrestle not against flesh and blood, but against principalities, against powers, against the rulers of the darkness of this world, against spiritual wickedness in high places. Wherefore take unto you the whole armour of God, that ye may be able to withstand in the evil day, and having done all, to stand. Stand therefore, having your loins girt about with truth, and having on the breastplate of righteousness; and your feet shod with the preparation of the gospel of peace; above all, taking the shield of faith, wherewith ye shall be able to quench all the fiery darts of the wicked. And take the helmet of salvation, and the sword of the Spirit, which is the word of God."*

Often we need direction. The longest chapter in the Bible, Psalm 119 is helpful. Verses like Psalms 119:9-11, *"Wherewithal shall a young man cleanse his way? By taking heed thereto according to thy word. With my whole heart have I sought thee: o let me not wander from thy commandments. Thy word have I hid in mine heart, that I might not sin against thee."* and 119:105, *"Thy word is a lamp unto my feet, and a light unto my path"* are typical of many wonderful passages.

There are those who talk much about grace and seem to divorce obedience from truth. Grace is all we can depend on for our salvation. This does not lead to a license to sin. Perish the thought!

In the Old Testament, there were ceremonial laws. In these laws there are principles. They teach us about the character of God. God's character does not change. As we search God's Word we find moral laws about who our God is. The purpose of the Bible is to know

God. Grace promotes love and such love promotes obedience unto Christ.

In chapter 1:14-25, Peter points out four elements of living out the grace life. They are the holiness of God (1:14-15), the Scripture (1:16, 23), the judgment of God (1:17) and the joy of God's family (1:22-25).

In addressing the holiness of God, Peter likens the followers of Christ to parents and their children. God has given to us the privilege to be partakers of His divine nature (II Peter 1:4).

Those who do not have Jesus Christ as their Savior lack knowledge. The ignorance is that their minds are fleshly with worldly indulgences. All individuals have a fallen nature that leads to sinful behavior. God's people, recipients of grace, need to exhibit that grace.

Peter utilizes a common New Testament word to describe this change. It is the word *"called."* We are called "out of darkness into His marvelous light" (I Peter 2:9). Jesus, Himself is the light (John 1:7-11). This light is reflected through the people of God. We are called to follow the Lord's example of humility. This is best recognized when we suffer (I Peter 2:21). Retaliation is not a practice for Christians. I Peter 3:9 states, *"Thy word is a lamp unto my feet, and a light unto my path."* Evil for evil is not a practice for God's children. We are, in fact, called to give and to inherit a blessing. The first epistle ends with a reminder that we are called to eternal glory. I Peter 5:10, *"But the God of all grace, who hath called us unto his eternal glory by Christ Jesus, after that ye have suffered a while, make you perfect, stablish, strengthen, settle you."*

The suffering of Christ is certainly a theme of I Peter. However, the glory of God is equally an ongoing theme of I Peter. The glory of God is not one of the attributes of God. It is the totality of all His attributes and all that God is. The glory of God is all that He is! He deserves all glory because He is almighty, omnipotent God. God has called us to Him. He is all wise, all seeking, and everywhere present. God's holiness is an essential truth that reflects the glory of God.

When we trust Jesus Christ as our Savior we are in position. God the Father sees us in His Son Jesus Christ. We are in Christ meaning our standing is in Him. Our holiness in practice comes from Him.

The word, sanctify means to be "set apart." As mentioned earlier, it has three tenses. It speaks of past sanctification meaning we were set apart to be God's at salvation. There is present sanctification meaning that we are progressively becoming like Him. Future sanctification is when we are with Him in heaven. Our holy life is for the purpose of bringing glory to God.

The second element in living out the grace life is the Scripture. Leviticus 11:44 declares, "You shall be holy, for I am holy." The question is simple, "What does the Bible say?" I Peter 1:23, *"Being born again, not of corruptible seed, but of incorruptible, by the word of God, which liveth and abideth for ever."* We are born again by the Word of God. God's Word will never decay, disappoint, disappear, nor become irrelevant. It is God's Word to us. Psalm 1:1-3, *"Peter, an apostle of Jesus Christ, to the strangers scattered throughout Pontus, Galatia, Cappadocia, Asia, and Bithynia, elect according to the foreknowledge of God the Father, through sanctification of the Spirit, unto obedience and sprinkling of the blood of Jesus Christ: Grace unto you, and peace, be multiplied. Blessed be the God and Father of our Lord Jesus Christ, which according to his abundant mercy hath begotten us again unto a lively hope by the resurrection of Jesus Christ from the dead."* The law of the Lord is God's precious word. We are to live in and by it. Holy living is obedience to God's word.

The third element is the judgment of God (1:17). It is difficult to get our arms around the love of God and the holiness of God. God loves us and He is holy. John 17:11, *"And now I am no more in the world, but these are in the world, and I come to thee. Holy Father, keep through thine own name those whom thou hast given me, that they may be one, as we are."* He will judge. Yet He is merciful, forgiving and loving. Peter writes here to believers. He is addressing the service and the works of "God's people. When our Lord returns there will be a time of judgment. Romans 14:10-12, *"But why dost thou judge thy brother? Or why dost thou set at nought thy brother? For we shall all stand before the judgment seat of Christ. For it is written, As I live, saith the Lord, every knee shall bow to me, and every tongue shall confess to God. So then every one of us shall give account of himself to God."* II Corinthians 5:9-10, *"Wherefore we labour, that, whether present or absent, we may be accepted of him. For we must all appear before the judgment seat of Christ; that every one may receive the things done in his body, according to that he hath done, whether it be good or bad."* God will reward His children at the judgment seat. *"Therefore judge nothing before the time, until the Lord come, who both will bring to light the hidden things of darkness, and will make manifest the counsels of the hearts: and then shall every man have praise of God."I Corinthians 4:5* One of the elements missing with so many people today is Godly fear. This does not mean a fear that produces fright but a godly respect for the Almighty. A loving child does not wish to disobey and disappoint their parents. Likewise, God's people desire to please their heavenly Father.

There are many Jewish friends who will not mention God's name out of respect. In our walk with God we need to remember His character and the joy of a holy life.

The passage concludes with an emphasis on the family of God (1:18-25). We need to remember what we were once like. We were slaves in need to be set free from condemnation. In first century Rome there were millions of slaves. A slave could earn enough money to buy freedom. The master could also sell the slave to someone who would pay the price and set him free. Many slaves felt at home and loved by their masters. If they wished to remain with the master, they could, or they would go somewhere of their choosing to be under another master. The gospel frees us and we have a new master.

We are in our nature slaves to sin. Slavery leads to an empty life. The happiness of this world cannot satisfy the longing in our spirits. The word redemption is best defined "to set someone free by the paying of a price." In salvation, only the blood of Jesus can redeem us. Throughout Peter's writings in I Peter he mentions the blood of Christ: *"For even hereunto were ye called: because Christ also suffered for us, leaving us an example, that ye should follow his steps"* (2:21); *"For Christ also hath once suffered for sins, the just for the unjust, that he might bring us to God, being put to death in the flesh, but quickened by the Spirit"* (3:18); *"The elders which are among you I exhort, who am also an elder, and a witness of the sufferings of Christ, and also a partaker of the glory that shall be revealed"* (5:1).

The reference to a lamb reminds these believers of the sacrifices of the Old Testament teaching of an innocent victim giving life for those who would deserve death. The Passover lamb was predictive of the Messiah who would die for the sins of the world (Exodus 12). When, John the Baptist saw the Lord, he exclaimed *"Behold the lamb of God, who takes away the sin of the world"* (John 1:29).

This death of Messiah was ordered by God. The death of Christ to casual observers would seem like a terrible waste but from God's perspective it was the Father's divine plan that was decided before the foundation of the world.

The old hymn says, "Hallelujah! What a Savior!" Truly He is! This love provides the experience of the new birth (vv. 23-25). We were born of the flesh. Now we are born of the spirit.

Peter uses two different and common words for love. Phileo is the word for *"brotherly love"* (Philadelphia), and the sacrificial God-like love is *"agape."* It took the miracle of God's love to provide salvation. As we live the Christ life we need to learn to love the brethren. This love is prompted by the Holy Spirit. He calls this unfeigned love which means without hypocrisy. Christian love is a matter of the will. God treats us and gives us what we do not deserve. We need to learn to treat others in a similar fashion.

In conclusion, we cannot live a holy life apart from the grace of God. The desire of a child of God needs to be to bring glory to Him. What a privilege and glorious honor!

Questions:
1. What does the word *'holy'* mean?
2. What are the three tenses of sanctification?
3. What do many of the Old Testament ceremonial laws teach us?
4. What are the four elements to living out the grace life?

Discussion:
1. What are some practical ways to live a clean (holy) life?

Chapter 4

LIVING AS A PRIEST
I Peter 2:1-10

"Wherefore laying aside all malice, and all guile, and hypocrisies, and envies, and all evil speakings, as newborn babes, desire the sincere milk of the word, that ye may grow thereby: if so be ye have tasted that the Lord is gracious. To whom coming, as unto a living stone, disallowed indeed of men, but chosen of God, and precious, ye also, as lively stones, are built up a spiritual house, an holy priesthood, to offer up spiritual sacrifices, acceptable to God by Jesus Christ. Wherefore also it is contained in the scripture, Behold, I lay in Sion a chief corner stone, elect, precious: and he that believeth on him shall not be confounded. Unto you therefore which believe he is precious: but unto them which be disobedient, the stone which the builders disallowed, the same is made the head of the corner, and a stone of stumbling, and a rock of offence, even to them which stumble at the word, being disobedient: whereunto also they were appointed. But ye are a chosen generation, a royal priesthood, an holy nation, a peculiar people; that ye should show forth the praises of him who hath called you out of darkness into his marvellous light; which in time past were not a people, but are now the people of God: which had not obtained mercy, but now have obtained mercy." **(I Peter 2:1-10)**

S ome years ago I led a truck driver to Christ who had a rather rough background. He went to the bookstore and bought several Bibles and commentaries, and one night he called me and asked me to come to his house. As I walked in the house, he immediately explained his dilemma.

"I don't know how to blankety-blank understand all of this," he said. Obviously, his language was still a bit raw at that time. At his house, he had all of these materials spread out on his table. It was frustrating to him that he did not know what to do with all of it.

He pointed out to me I Pet. 1:15-16. *"But as he which hath called you is holy, so be ye holy in all manner of conversation; Because it is written, Be ye holy; for I am holy."*

This man who had been saved only a short time looked right at me and asked, "How in the blankety-blank am I supposed to be holy?"

"That really is a good question," I answered.

When you think about being holy compared to God, it is easy to wonder how in the world we could ever accomplish that. That is the theme that connects the latter half of chapter 1 with the opening verses of chapter 2; God is saying to us here that He wants holy people, and He reminds us what it means to be holy.

On one of my trips to Israel I was at the church in Nazareth with the group I had brought over from the United States. An evangelist was on that trip and we were talking in front of the church when a priest came through very quickly and almost knocked the evangelist off his feet.

We looked at our guide. "Can he do that?" we asked.

The guide shrugged. "He is the priest," he said. "He can do whatever he wants to do." So does a priest have such rights?

A priest is a special person held in high regard among his followers. The Word of God tells us in this passage that we are priests, which means we have a special relationship with the Lord.

In the Old Testament there were five basic things that a priest did. First, he was the one who modeled God. People looked at him and said, "This is the person in our midst who is most like God." The priest was a representative of God.

Second, he represented the truth. This made people want to hear what he had to say.

Third, the priest was an intercessor, which meant he was a go-between with the people and God when it came to making sacrifices, etc.

Fourth, he spoke for God. When God said something, the people came to listen to priests and find out what God said. Finally, he was to be a servant of God.

I have found that when most people are saved, regardless of their age or their past, Satan tries to make us believe that we are not worth much at all. We need to tell Satan to go right back where he belongs. God tells us in His Word that we are part of the royal priesthood – not just "a" priesthood, but "the" royal priesthood.

We can now look at the passage in I Peter and see how the five elements of an Old Testament priest are the ingredients of the priesthood in your life.

We see the first point in I Pet. 1:18-19. *"Forasmuch as ye know that ye were not redeemed with corruptible things, as silver and gold, from your vain conversation received by tradition from your fathers; But with the precious blood of Christ, as of a lamb without blemish and without spot."*

The word *"redeemed"* was commonly used during this time as people were often bought and sold as slaves. Verse 18 talks about the currencies used typically to make such purchases, and *"vain conversation"* refers to the rabbinical traditions of the day. Verse 19 shows that we model God because the blood of His Son cleanses us from all of our sin.

When you stand before God the Father as His child and He looks at you, He sees you as if you had never committed a sin. This is not because of any merit or goodness on your part, but because of the precious blood of Jesus Christ.

This theme is presented throughout the Bible. Revelation 1:5-6 says, *"And from Jesus Christ, who is the faithful witness, and the first begotten of the dead, and the prince of the kings of the earth. Unto him that loved us, and washed us from our sins in his own blood, And hath made us kings and priests unto God and his Father; to him be glory and dominion forever and ever. Amen."*

Look at the picture of Heaven portrayed in Revelation 5:9-10. "*And they sung a new song, saying, Thou art worthy to take the book, and to open the seals thereof: for thou wast slain, and hast redeemed us to God by thy blood out of every kindred, and tongue, and people, and nation; And hast made us unto our God kings and priests: and we shall reign on the earth.*"

The blood from the veins of the Son of God is the blood of God Himself. Jesus Christ was virgin-born. His mother was Mary and Joseph was his stepfather. Because His blood came from God the Father, it was divine blood that was shed for us. We know from the book of Leviticus as well as modern medical science that "*the life of the flesh is in the blood*" (Lev. 17:11).

The Bible says in Ephesians 1:7, "*In whom we have redemption through his blood, the forgiveness of sins, according to the riches of his grace.*"

This amazing plan was conceived before the world began, according to I Pet. 1:20. "*Who verily was foreordained before the foundation of the world, but was manifest in these last times for you.*" People talk about their good works and how they try to please God, but God is pleased by His Son. Because He only sees Christ when He looks at us, we should have a relationship in which we become more and more in love with Him every day.

You may notice that when a couple has been married a long time, each person begins to look more like his or her spouse. The same goes for our resemblance to our parents as we get older. A man who knew my father told me recently that I look more like my dad, and I consider that a compliment. We become more and more like the ones we love.

A lady was preparing a ham for some guests one day and she cut off both ends of the ham. Her guest asked, "Why did you do that?"

"That's the way you prepare a ham," was the reply.

"No, it's not. Where did you learn that?"

"My mother taught me to do that."

The guest was acquainted with her mother, and she asked her why her daughter prepared a ham that way. "My mother taught me that," the older lady said.

The grandmother was still alive, and when she was asked about her preferred method for preparing a ham, she said, "The pan was only so big. I had to cut the ends off."

This woman had taught her daughter, who in turn taught her own daughter, until all of them did it the same way. They were very much alike.

I love to go fishing. When I moved to south Florida, there was a man in my church there who was a professional fisherman.

"Pastor, I'm going to take you out to the Everglades," he said to me. "We're going to catch bass like you've never seen before."

We went out on a speed boat and saw alligators and other wildlife as we traveled to our fishing spot. Once we arrived, it was time to fish. I started putting a worm on my hook when he said, "That's not the way you do that."

"Yes, it is," I replied.

We went back and forth for a moment before I realized I was debating this point with a professional fisherman. I was baiting my hook the way my father had taught me, and although I did not catch as many fish as my friend did, I baited the hook the way I wanted to. That was simply a way I identified with my late father.

When we read I Peter 1:16 which tells us, *"Be ye holy; for I am holy,"* we are not being instructed to follow some particular set of rules or standards. This is an admonition to live our lives more like the One who models holiness for us, who is the Lord Jesus Christ.

Now let's move to the next point, which is how the priest reveals the truth of God. Look at verse 22. *"Seeing ye have purified your souls in obeying the truth through the Spirit unto unfeigned love of the brethren, see that ye love one another with a pure heart fervently."* This verse suggests a special relationship with each other that is based upon the truth.

Verse 23 says, *"Being born again, not of corruptible seed, but of incorruptible, by the word of God, which lives and abides forever."* The source of that truth is revealed in this verse.

The next two verses remind us of the temporal nature of our lives in comparison to the eternal Word of God. *"For all flesh is as grass, and all the glory of man as the flower of grass. The grass withereth, and the flower thereof falleth away: But the word of the*

Lord endureth for ever. And this is the word which by the gospel is preached unto you."

The word in verse 23 for *"word"* is the Greek word *logos*, which in essence means "the written word." In verse 25 the Greek word is *rama*, which means "the spoken word."

In either form, you and I represent the truth of Jesus Christ because we are the priests of God, having been chosen by Him into His wonderful family upon the acceptance of Christ in our lives. It is one thing to love the Word of God and proclaim it in the pulpit and worship Him corporately, but the way we project His Word through our lives beyond the four walls of the church will really determine whether others receive the truth they so desperately need.

I was a pastor for nearly a year before I led an adult to Christ for the first time. I had led children and teens to Christ but never an adult. When I was still a college student I asked my pastor if I could get some church buses and bring in some children for Vacation Bible School. He said I could, so I filled two buses with children from a nearby housing project.

I did not notify the VBS teachers in advance and they had no idea what they would do with all of these children. So I took them to a park.

"What are we going to do," a friend of mine asked.

"Let's tell them about Jesus," I said.

We led 22 children to Christ that day. That was an exciting day. I remember thinking after it was over that I needed to tell more people about Jesus.

I remember the first couple I led to Christ. Their names were Tom and Martha. I went to visit them after they came to our church. I had memorized everything you could ever want to know about the plan of salvation, and I was scared to death.

"If you died today, do you know you would go to Heaven?" I asked.

"No," they replied.

"Would you like to know?"

"Yes, we would."

I was dumbfounded. "You would?" I replied. For a moment I didn't know what to say.

They were gloriously saved that day and later baptized in our church. They served the Lord for many years and today they are in Heaven.

As a priest using the description in I Peter, I have a responsibility to point people to Jesus. You have the same responsibility. Not everyone is going to accept Christ and we are not concerned with numbers so much as the idea that we continue to represent the truth.

The third attribute of the priest is intercession, and as we consider that point let's look at verse 1 of chapter 2, which tells us about *"laying aside all malice, and all guile, and hypocrisies, and envies, and all evil speakings."* Obviously there are things here that God does not want us to have in our lives.

Verse 2 says, *"As newborn babes, desire the sincere milk of the word, that ye may grow thereby: If so be ye have tasted that the Lord is gracious."* That describes the way our attitude should be toward the things of God and our desire to know more about Him. The word *"gracious"* here reinforces our point from a previous chapter that God is a good God.

It is a wonderful privilege to function as intercessors – praying for one another, thinking about one another, caring for one another, doing for one another – just as Jesus intercedes for us with God the Father.

The fourth duty of an Old Testament priest was so speak for God. With that in mind, notice the analogy in verses 4-5. *"To whom coming, as unto a living stone, disallowed indeed of men, but chosen of God, and precious, Ye also, as lively stones, are built up a spiritual house, an holy priesthood, to offer up spiritual sacrifices, acceptable to God by Jesus Christ."* The Lord is pictured as a stone, and we are pictured as living stones.

In Matthew 16 we see a conversation Jesus had with His disciples after they had been living and traveling with Him for some time. Look at verses 13-18.

"When Jesus came into the coasts of Caesarea Philippi, he asked his disciples, saying, Whom do men say that I the Son of man am? And they said, Some say that thou art John the Baptist: some, Elias; and others, Jeremias, or one of the prophets. He saith unto them, But whom say ye that I am? And Simon Peter answered and said, Thou

art the Christ, the Son of the living God. And Jesus answered and said unto him, Blessed art thou, Simon Barjona: for flesh and blood hath not revealed it unto thee, but my Father which is in heaven. And I say also unto thee, That thou art Peter, and upon this rock I will build my church; and the gates of hell shall not prevail against it."

Satan may have some power and some authority, but he is no match whatsoever for the Lord Jesus Christ. Many times the devil tells us how bad things are, how weak we are, or how we cannot do this or that. This passage reminds us not only of the power of God, but also what we can do for Him when we allow Him to use us.

As we go back to I Peter, consider a familiar story relating to the building of the temple. The corner stone was sent ahead from the quarry but was rejected by the builders as not being the right one. When it came time to set it, they were chagrined as the corner stone sat lying in the weeds. It was the most important piece of all. However it was rejected.

Just as the stone was rejected, we see in verse 4 that Christ was rejected by men, as he often is. In 40 years as a pastor I saw many people in church who could not wait for me to stop preaching because they wanted so badly to be saved. Others wanted me to stop preaching because they did not understand any of it and couldn't care less. There are many who thoroughly reject Jesus and want nothing to do with Him.

A few years ago I participated in a roundtable discussion at England's Oxford University. Among the other panelists there was an atheist and evolutionist. He was a brilliant man. Like the other Christians in attendance, I was friendly with him, and he was friendly as well until the conversation moved toward anything having to do with God. He wanted no part of that. He simply rejected it!

As we think about the frequent rejection of Christ, consider verse 6. *"Wherefore also it is contained in the scripture, Behold, I lay in Sion a chief corner stone, elect, precious: and he that believeth on him shall not be confounded."* This is a direct reference to Isaiah 28:16, which says, *"Therefore thus saith the Lord GOD, Behold, I lay in Zion for a foundation a stone, a tried stone, a precious corner stone, a sure foundation: he that believeth shall not make haste."*

The word *"confounded"* in verse 6 is also translated as "ashamed." You will never have to worry about being ashamed, disappointed or let down because of Jesus. Verse 7 goes on state the value of this corner stone: *"Unto you therefore which believe he is precious: but unto them which be disobedient, the stone which the builders disallowed, the same is made the head of the corner."* The stone which was originally thrown into the rubble is priceless. There is none other like it. That is an apt description of our Savior.

Look at verse 8. *"And a stone of stumbling, and a rock of offence, even to them which stumble at the word, being disobedient: whereunto also they were appointed."* The word *"stumbling"* here is the same word from which we get our word "scandal." God is saying here that some will stumble to the point of thinking it a scandal that Jesus Christ could be the only way of salvation. Today in the United States there are many people who say, "Have your faith and enjoy it, but do not criticize the way I believe." We are told not to proselyte and attempt to bring people into the family of God, but that is the exact opposite of the commission our Lord has given us. In that instance, we should obey God rather than man.

This brings us to the fifth and final point regarding a priest, which is serving God. Look at the marvelous promise in verse 9. *"But ye are a chosen generation, a royal priesthood, an holy nation, a peculiar people; that ye should show forth the praises of him who hath called you out of darkness into his marvellous light."*

As *"a chosen generation,"* we belong to a very special group of people. My father told me often how important the Pedrone name was and that I should not ever do anything to bring shame to that name. I have not forgotten that.

In the Old Testament we had the priesthood of Aaron. This *"royal priesthood"* is different; it is the direct lineage of the Lord Jesus Christ.

The *"holy nation"* refers to a people group, as the Greek word here is *ethos*, from which we get "ethnic." As a *"peculiar people"* we are not odd but very special and of great value.

There is only one high priest, and that is our Lord and Savior Jesus Christ. But we are part of a royal priesthood. When you live a clean and pure life for God, He puts an anointing on your life that other people do not have. That is a special touch of God for the task that He has given you. You and I who name the name of Jesus Christ – who know the Lord and want to live for Him – need to understand that we are members of royalty.

My wife and I were in the Tower of London waiting all day to see the Crown Jewels. A guard was telling us, "Keep moving," and we almost missed them as we walked by. I went back in again, but this time I walked slower because I wanted to see the jewels.

As children of God, you and I are crown jewels to Him. God can greatly use our lives if we allow Him to do so.

We are members of a royal priesthood. We are a chosen generation. We are to live holy as He is holy. The way to do that is by getting closer to Him every day.

Questions:
1. What are the five basic things an Old Testament priest did?
2. What does "*peculiar people*" mean?
3. There are two Greek words used in this chapter for "*word*". What are they and what do they mean?

Discussion
1. Describe biblically about what it means to be a chosen generation.

Chapter 5

SUBMISSION IN A WORLD OF ENTITLEMENT
I Peter 2:11-25

"Dearly beloved, I beseech you as strangers and pilgrims, abstain from fleshly lusts, which war against the soul; having your conversation honest among the Gentiles: that, whereas they speak against you as evildoers, they may by your good works, which they shall behold, glorify God in the day of visitation. Submit yourselves to every ordinance of man for the Lord's sake: whether it be to the king, as supreme; or unto governors, as unto them that are sent by him for the punishment of evildoers, and for the praise of them that do well. For so is the will of God, that with well doing ye may put to silence the ignorance of foolish men: as free, and not using your liberty for a cloke of maliciousness, but as the servants of God. Honour all men. Love the brotherhood. Fear God. Honour the king. Servants, be subject to your masters with all fear; not only to the good and gentle, but also to the froward. For this is thankworthy, if a man for conscience toward God endure grief, suffering wrongfully. For what glory is it, if, when ye be buffeted for your faults, ye shall take it patiently? But if, when ye do well, and suffer for it, ye take it patiently, this is acceptable with God. For even hereunto were ye called: because Christ also suffered for us, leaving us an example, that ye should follow his steps: who did no sin, neither was guile

found in his mouth: who, when he was reviled, reviled not again; when he suffered, he threatened not; but committed himself to him that judgeth righteously: who his own self bare our sins in his own body on the tree, that we, being dead to sins, should live unto righteousness: by whose stripes ye were healed. For ye were as sheep going astray; but are now returned unto the Shepherd and Bishop of your souls." **(I Peter 2:11-25)**

*A*s an American, I am quick to comment that I love America. It is truly a great nation. We have a flaw that could, however, destroy the fabric of freedom. It is contained in the word *"entitlement."* Entitlement means there are things owed to me! The question then as a Christian is what are my entitlements? This section of Peter's epistle reverses the entitlement concept to emphasize the importance of living a submissive life. He does it in four areas: a citizen (2:11-17); as an employee (2:18-29); in marriage (3:1-7); and as a part of the church (3:8-12).

Submission recognizes the supremacy, authority, and leadership of God in my life. There are three reasons in this section to submit to the Lordship of our triune God in this passage.

The Example to the Lost – I Peter 2:11-17

The first reason for submission is because the lost world needs to see a change in the believer in order to be drawn to Jesus Christ. The epistle reminds us that God loves us. Throughout the two epistles there is this reminder. I Peter 2:11 says, *"Dearly beloved, I beseech you as strangers and pilgrims, abstain from fleshly lusts, which war against the soul."* I Peter 4:12, *"Beloved, think it not strange concerning the fiery trial which is to try you, as though some strange thing happened unto you."*

Look at the following passages in II Peter: *"And to godliness brotherly kindness; and to brotherly kindness charity"* (1:7); *"This second epistle, beloved, I now write unto you; in both which I stir up your pure minds by way of remembrance"* (3:1); *"But, beloved, be not ignorant of this one thing, that one day is with the Lord as a thousand years, and a thousand years as one day"* (3:8); *"Wherefore, beloved, seeing that ye look for such things, be diligent that ye may be found of him in peace, without spot, and blameless. And account that the longsuffering of our Lord is salvation; even as our beloved brother Paul also according to the wisdom given unto him hath written unto you"* (3:14-15); *"Ye therefore, beloved, seeing ye know these things before, beware lest ye also, being led away with the error of the wicked, fall from your own stedfastness"* (3:17).

God's love is His choice. He has chosen us for heaven. We are actually permanent citizens of another land. We are strangers and pilgrims passing through this land. Remember, Peter is writing to those of the diaspara. He uses the term "Gentiles" as a reminder of the unsaved. There is a spiritual war going on! The unsaved are observing how Christians live. Christians need to be aboveboard. We need to be honest. This word speaks about more than telling the truth. It is a concept of being admirable. There should be a spiritual attractiveness about the people of God.

I pastored for forty years. I had the honor of shepherding many wonderful followers of Christ. As any pastor would experience there were always people who constantly were difficult because their expectations were all about their personal desires. We need to follow Christ and be a witness to those who are without the Savior so that what we say and do will match each other.

In the Work Force – I Peter 2:13-17

Submission to government takes on many questions. Freedom in Peter's world was limited. In America our freedom is to be a government for the people. We have the privilege to elect leaders and the people speak with their vote in this representative government. The word "ordinance" means institution. We are to submit to the institutions that make the laws. I am sure Peter remembered when the Jewish council told the disciples to stop preaching in the name of Jesus. The disciples refused. Look at Acts 4:19, *"But Peter and John answered and said unto them, Whether it be right in the sight of God to hearken unto you more than unto God, judge ye"* and Acts 5:29, *"Then Peter and the other apostles answered and said, We ought to obey God rather than men."*

It is interesting to note that they kept preaching but did not cause a rebellion. There are occasions when leaders are placed in authority and it would appear that they are difficult to respect. The Christian approach should be to honor the office for all authority has been ordained by God (Romans 13:1-7). The law of government, however, should never cause us to go against God's law and therefore our conscience would be violated.

As a pastor and then a college president there were many occasions that building codes, safety issues, health issues, and protection of certain properties or people were to be enforced and it was Biblically correct to obey these areas as long as we could preach truth and operate our business under the authority of God.

The king here means "emperor." Peter did not recommend the overthrow of the government or the emperor. The governors refer to lawmakers.

Notice the phrase "the will of God" in verse 15. God wants the critics of the gospel to see the example of those who are servants that do good. This will lessen and even possibly silence those who verbally criticize.

Remember our freedom is in Christ but it does not give us an entitlement. Freedom is not for warfare with the world but to attract the unsaved.

Peter on several occasions talked about "loving the brotherhood". Look at the following verses in I Peter: *"Seeing ye have purified your souls in obeying the truth through the Spirit unto unfeigned love of the brethren, see that ye love one another with a pure heart fervently"* (1:22); *"Finally, be ye all of one mind, having compassion one of another, love as brethren, be pitiful, be courteous"* (3:8); *"And above all things have fervent charity among yourselves: for charity shall cover the multitude of sins"* (4:8); *"Greet ye one another with a kiss of charity. Peace be with you all that are in Christ Jesus. Amen"* (5:14). We honor and love the brotherhood by our example of submission to the powers that be.

"Fear God" and "honor the King" are attitudes we need to develop. This does not mean we should not make use of our citizenship. It means we should respect the authority. It is wise and good to enter into the world of government and to be involved. But we should always be a part of a Christian community that respects the positions of leadership.

Beginning in verse 18, Peter addresses Christian slaves. We do not have slavery in America. History has accounts of Christians like Wilber Wilberforce in England, who fought against the terrible world of slavery. Slavery was a terrible episode in America's history. The application deals with attitude and application where we work. There is a strong tendency to fight and demand rights. Anyone can fight! In Ephesians 5:18 the Scripture commands us to be ". . .filled with the Spirit". One such relationship is the work force in Ephesians 6. It takes a spirit filled life to submit! In the writing of the epistles there is doctrine following by responsibility. It is very tempting to fight! Peter knew this. He was the disciple who led the way to stop Jesus crucifixion. When he finally realized his error he thought it was too late!

When there are laws that strike our conscience we are to obey God rather than man. But we must not do it for our entitlement sake!

The section closes with Jesus presented as our example (2:21-23); sacrifice (2:24) and the bishop of our souls (2:25).

Jesus is our example. He suffered in word and deed. We need a Savior! We need an example. His example does not save us! He is an example and our perfect mentor.

As our Savior, He took our sins in His own body on the cross. It is interesting to notice that Jewish people did not crucify unless the criminal was considered very dangerous and evil. Deuteronomy 21:23 says, *"His body shall not remain all night upon the tree, but thou shalt in any wise bury him that day; (for he that is hanged is accursed of God;) that thy land be not defiled, which the LORD thy God giveth thee for an inheritance."* Likewise in the New testament book of Galatians 3:13, *"Christ hath redeemed us from the curse of the law, being made a curse for us: for it is written, Cursed is every one that hangeth on a tree."*

He is the bishop or overseer of our souls. The Great Shepherd died for the sheep. Isaiah 53:3-6 says, *"He is despised and rejected of men; a man of sorrows, and acquainted with grief: and we hid as it were our faces from him; he was despised, and we esteemed him not. Surely he hath borne our griefs, and carried our sorrows: yet we did esteem him stricken, smitten of God, and afflicted. But he was wounded for our transgressions, he was bruised for our iniquities: the chastisement of our peace was upon him; and with his stripes we are healed. All we like sheep have gone astray; we have turned every one to his own way; and the Lord hath laid on him the iniquity of us all."* We are all like wandering sheep. We are separated from God. He is the bishop who oversees the flock.

The lost world will see Jesus in us. He works everything together for His glory and we are to submit in order to win some.

Questions:
1. What are some reasons believers should submit to government?
2. Why did Peter say, "We ought to obey God rather than men?"

Discussion:
1. What are some issues that would cause a believer to disobey the government's authority?

Chapter 6

SUBMISSION IN A MARRAIGE
I Peter 3:1-7

"Likewise, ye wives, be in subjection to your own husbands; that, if any obey not the word, they also may without the word be won by the conversation of the wives; while they behold your chaste conversation coupled with fear. Whose adorning let it not be that outward adorning of plaiting the hair, and of wearing of gold, or of putting on of apparel; but let it be the hidden man of the heart, in that which is not corruptible, even the ornament of a meek and quiet spirit, which is in the sight of God of great price. For after this manner in the old time the holy women also, who trusted in God, adorned themselves, being in subjection unto their own husbands: even as Sara obeyed Abraham, calling him lord: whose daughters ye are, as long as ye do well, and are not afraid with any amazement. Likewise, ye husbands, dwell with them according to knowledge, giving honour unto the wife, as unto the weaker vessel, and as being heirs together of the grace of life; that your prayers be not hindered." **(I Peter 3:1-7)**

*T*here is a plethora of information on marriage. Radio shows, Christian television, books, seminars, pamphlets and various forms of material appear through electronic media. Christian marriages are challenging. The culture of the Western world makes it more difficult. Marriage, quite frankly, is not presented as a popular relationship.

The Apostle Peter in I Peter 3:1-7 addresses the situation specifically from the standpoint of a Christian wife who has an unsaved husband. The teaching of the passage is very helpful in all areas of marriage. It appears to me that the key word in this section is, again, the word 'submission' found in verses one and five. The term is a military term that means "to place under rank". The Scripture pictures the husband as the head of the home because it illustrates the greater relationship of Christ's headship over the church. Ephesians 5:21-33 says, *"Submitting yourselves one to another in the fear of God. Wives, submit yourselves unto your own husbands, as unto the Lord. For the husband is the head of the wife, even as Christ is the head of the church: and he is the savior of the body. Therefore as the church is subject unto Christ, so let the wives be to their own husbands in everything. Husbands, love your wives, even as Christ also loved the church, and gave himself for it; that he might sanctify and cleanse it with the washing of water by the word, that he might present it to himself a glorious church, not having spot, or wrinkle, or any such thing; but that it should be holy and without blemish. So ought men to love their wives as their own bodies. He that loveth his wife loveth himself. For no man ever yet hated his own flesh; but nourisheth and cherisheth it, even as the Lord the church: for we are members of his body, of his flesh, and of his bones. For this cause shall a man leave his father and mother, and shall be joined unto his wife, and they two shall be one flesh. This is a great mystery: but I speak concerning Christ and the church. Nevertheless let every one of you in particular so love his wife even as himself; and the wife see that she reverence her husband."*

It is at the point of headship where there is an issue. God has placed authority in an order. Headship is not a Hitler-like dictatorship. The husband's leadership is under the authority of the lordship of Jesus Christ. As Christ loved the church the husband is to love his wife.

Marriage must be worked at. The first word in verse 1 is *"likewise."* The concept is "in the same manner" or "in like manner." There is a precedent to the meaning. The precedent goes back to I

Peter 2:21-25 where we are taught that Jesus was submissive to the Father, *"For even hereunto were ye called: because Christ also suffered for us, leaving us an example, that ye should follow his steps: who did no sin, neither was guile found in his mouth: who, when he was reviled, reviled not again; when he suffered, he threatened not; but committed himself to him that judgeth righteously: who his own self bare our sins in his own body on the tree, that we, being dead to sins, should live unto righteousness: by whose stripes ye were healed. For ye were as sheep going astray; but are now returned unto the Shepherd and Bishop of your souls."*

An obvious question for men is, "How well do you know your wife?" Men often love their wives but do not notice their wives' feelings. Most women have emotional issues that come from both physical and emotional needs. A wife needs to be able to speak to her husband. Husbands are usually quick to try to "fix" something, when wives simply want someone listen to them. Communication is vital. Most Saturday mornings my wife and I sit, drink coffee, and chat. We both agree those couple of hours together are some of our "favorites" Find time to enjoy chatting together. It is therapeutic!

The first verse of I Peter 3 says, *"Likewise, ye wives, be in subjection to your own husbands; that, if any obey not the word, they also may without the word be won by the conversation of the wives."* God wants us to have a happy and fulfilling marriage. Men and women are one in Christ and therefore on the same level. In the world of employment numerous women have to work and therefore they should be paid the same as any man for the job of equal work. In our salvation men and women are equal in Christ. In Roman days there were slaves who were professionals and experts in various fields. They were, however, under authority. Submission to authority is one of the first steps in learning how to strengthen character. Competition is not the purpose of marriage. The old song classic of America, "I can do anything better than you" separates a couple. In marriage it is "ours" not mine and yours. If there is a head there needs to be a body. A body without a head is incomplete and a head without a body is incomplete. The two parts, head and body, need to work together. When there is a single parent home the parent functions as both. There are many men and women who are amazingly strong in Christ as the parent raises their children alone Someone once said "what is my partner's is mine and what is mine is mine too." This is not God's direction in this passage. Additionally, pastors and Christian parents are wise to instruct and children to marry "in the faith" (II Corinthians 6:14-18).

The Platform to Win Someone to Christ is a Godly Life!

It Provides the Inner Glamour – I Peter 3:3-6

The Apostle Peter warns wives to major on her character within. The word for adorning is a Greek term that speaks of order and it is the opposite of chaotic behavior. In the Roman world women were very interested in the latest designs. Unfortunately the latest designs were utilized to "show off" to other women how up to date the fashion was and how expensive the clothing was. Peter is not speaking against nice clothing or even expensive garments. He is speaking about where true beauty lies. The clothing of the present will be out of style soon. True beauty comes from the inner life of a child of God.

Likewise Peter is not stating that women should not wear jewelry. He is speaking against the "showing off" of jewelry. Beauty does not need to be only skin deep but spirit deep. Of course women should look attractive and be careful of their health and appearance. But this is not the principle that will bring someone to Jesus Christ.

Sarah called Abram, lord. This was in keeping with their culture. Wives should "do good" by loving and caring for their unsaved husbands. In my many years of ministry I have had numerous couples come to Christ where one spouse was unsaved. This is not a guarantee but the principles can be lived with. This makes for the best arrangement, provides the best platform and the inner spirit is the inner glamour that is needed.

Christ is the example we should follow!

The teaching appears to be directed to the women. The reason deals with the woman's position in the Roman Expire. Women were inferior to the rank of man in the Roman Empire. Many of the Christian women were facing the challenge of their new found faith.

The question was this. How do I live in order to win my unsaved husband to Jesus Christ?

Sarah is the example to follow. Sarah showed her imperfections many times. Her suggestion to Abram to have a child with Hagar has produced an incredible family feud of the Jewish/Arab conflict for centuries. However, it is interesting to note that she is listed in Hebrews 11, the great Hall of Faith chapter. *"Through faith also Sara herself received strength to conceive seed, and was delivered of a child when she was past age, because she judged him faithful who had promised. Therefore sprang there even of one, and him as good as dead, so many as the stars of the sky in multitude, and as the sand which is by the sea shore innumerable"* (Hebrew 11:11-12). We are all sinners but Sarah's submission to Abram to provide a child in old age is unique and an example of what the Scriptures teach.

Giving Honor unto the Wife

Sarah's name means "princess." I would suggest that husbands go a step beyond that and recognize her as a queen. The "weaker vessel" here, I believe speaks to the position of the woman where, in the garden, she was taken from the rib of Adam. Although some commentators sense this refers to physical strength it seems to me to be a position again of a man's authority to protect his wife and family. Women may be stronger intellectually, emotionally and spiritually and sometimes even physically but it is a reference to the husband's position of protecting his wife.

One day I came home and my wife was on the telephone and it was obviously a tense situation. She kept waving at me to be quiet and I did something I seldom do. I picked up the extension line. My wife was talking to a man about a business situation she was taking care of for our family and he was rude and harsh. Being an Italian a flow of blood took off in me and I immediately "went off" on him demanding that I was coming to confront him. He lived hours away and it would probably be impossible to do so. He immediately backed down and apologized! Afterwards I thought to myself, "Did I do the right thing?" According to this passage it was the only thing to do.

Dwell with Them

Husbands have a responsibilty to spend time with their wives. My precious wife, Bobbi, and I are empty-nesters. I travel on behalf of Davis College about 50 Sundays every year to preach in churches and to speak at many Bible and Pastor's conferences. The great joy is she is with me. When I am at the office we usually connect once or twice and usually at the end of our conversations we say "I love you" to each other. Often she tells me how she likes just having me around. As men we need to understand how important that is! The "dwell with them" of this passage is addressing a fundamental need to be with each other. This speaks about every area from being in the same room quietly saying nothing to each other to traveling together and includes in-depth sexual relationships.

When the first child is born in a family it is very easy for the child to "come between" the parents. I believe and strongly recommend that men put in their schedules weekly private and quiet time with their spouse.

Often ministry people get so busy they do not take time together with their families.

An added biblical principle is that the man provide for the physical, material, and financial needs of the home. Although many wives work, their primary responsibility is the care of the home (Titus 2:4-5). If wives preach, nag, instruct, remind, and even threaten husbands with words it may turn him away from the Lord. "Without the word" means to live out the word by a lifestyle. It is the quiet, meek character that is lived out in a conduct of caring, concern, and love that will provide what the husband needs. This attitude must be real, not fake. Husbands need encouragement. Unfortunately men have a lot of pride and need huge encouragement. When they are encouraged and see in their wives' lives the encouragement they are apt to come to Jesus Christ as their Savior.

That Your Prayers be not Hindered

Are you having a hard time getting your prayers answered? Husbands and wives need to pray together. They are "heirs together". To lack a prayer life together is often to rob each other of blessing and growth. Spend time daily praying as a couple. When you fail don't go on guilt trips but pray faithfully together.

This is a wonderful section to check out with our marriage. Marriage is a wonderful blessing from Almighty God.

Questions:
1. What can hinder our prayer lives?
2. How is the wife the 'weaker vessel'?
3. What is your opinion of women wearing jewelry and fancy clothing? How does it compare to Peter's teaching?

Discussion
1. Make a list of unsaved people to pray for that you will begin a process of witnessing to.

Chapter 7

LOVING LIFE AND SEEING GOOD DAYS
I Peter 3:8-13

"Finally, be ye all of one mind, having compassion one of another, love as brethren, be pitiful, be courteous: not rendering evil for evil, or railing for railing: but contrariwise blessing; knowing that ye are thereunto called, that ye should inherit a blessing. For he that will love life, and see good days, let him refrain his tongue from evil, and his lips that they speak no guile: let him eschew evil, and do good; let him seek peace, and ensue it. For the eyes of the Lord are over the righteous, and his ears are open unto their prayers: but the face of the Lord is against them that do evil. And who is he that will harm you, if ye be followers of that which is good?" **(I Peter 3:8-13)**

S everal years ago I had a week that was like very few weeks in my entire life.

When I was a pastor in South Florida, we were invited to have New Testament Baptist Church Night at Pro Player Stadium in Miami during a Florida Marlins baseball game. This was the same year the Marlins won the World Series (2003). My wife and I, along with some other people from the church, sat in a private box. I had the privilege of throwing out the first pitch that night (after practicing for several days to make sure I got the ball over the plate without embarrassing myself).

That same week included two major life events for my family – my daughter got married, and my wife was scheduled to have cancer surgery. It is hard to imagine a more dramatic one-week swing from the heights of joy to the depths of despair than what surrounded those three events. However, there was more.

My brother, who had just gone through some cancer treatments, called me at the time of my wife's surgery to see how things were going. He was a very successful businessman in Rochester, New York. He was my only brother and had actually had some success as an actor off-Broadway when he was a young man. He was a brilliant man.

We talked for a few minutes and he asked how my wife was doing. Later that same night, I received a call from someone telling me that my brother had been in a fire. Not having all of the details at the time, I assumed it wasn't too serious. I found out that the stove had exploded in his kitchen and, after guiding another family member to safety outside, he became disoriented due to smoke inhalation and went the wrong way instead of exiting the house. The next day he was in eternity.

Two days after that, my new son-in-law's grandfather was walking into a garage with a screwdriver in his hand. He fell on it and in a matter of days passed away. I learned the next day that the wife of one of our preacher boys was on a plane bound for the Bahamas that crashed, and she died.

I wouldn't go so far to consider that a Job-type experience, but it was an interesting week to say the least. I remember a friend of mine driving eight or ten hours to be with me and help me that week, and he told me, "Be sure to focus on the right things." In the midst of this turmoil, as I had to consider my wife and daughter and everything else going on that, was the best advice I could have received.

The passage that begins in I Pet. 3:8 is the start of a section of the book of I Peter that deals with suffering. Many of you can think of circumstances in your own lives that were similar to what I have just described. It is sometimes easy to forget the battle that is constantly raging in the life of every Christian. The apostle Peter reminds us of this in I Peter 5:8. *"Be sober, be vigilant; because your adversary the devil, as a roaring lion, walketh about, seeking whom he may devour."*

The devil is very real, and we must never forget that. He has a purpose in our lives. We are warned in Ephesians 4:27, *"Neither give place to the devil."* Another warning is in II Timothy 2:26, which says, *"And that they may recover themselves out of the snare of the devil, who are taken captive by him at his will."* I John 3:8 teaches about *"the works of the devil."*

There is a struggle that goes on constantly, and it all comes down to what is in our minds. It's about what we are thinking. This is why I Peter 3:8 tells us, *"be ye all of one mind."* Have you ever noticed how you can have one thing on your mind that you just cannot shake loose, no matter how busy things are around you?

Several years ago my wife and I got a letter from the IRS that we owed an exorbitant amount of money. I connected with my accountant, who told me, "Everything is going to be fine. Don't worry about it." I thought, "That's easy for you to say."

As time went on I received more letters from the IRS and my accountant still told me it would all be fine. This went on for about a year. I wish I could tell you I didn't worry about it that entire time, but I did. Sometimes, it was the last thing I thought about before I went to sleep at night and the first thing I thought about in the morning when I woke up. Eventually it turned ought exactly as my accountant predicted.

There is always something to preoccupy your mind. It could be a health issue with yourself or a family member (as I mentioned regarding my wife's cancer surgery). We have all experienced things like that. You go on vacation to get a week of freedom from your day-to-day concerns, and it only takes one phone call to change everything.

I have a friend in Florida who I will call from time to time. When I ask him how he is doing, his response is always the same: "I'm loving life." He has never told me anything different. That is what Peter is encouraging us to do in these verses, even in the face of suffering. Let's look at four things we should consider that will help us live this way.

Consider the **MOTIVATION**. Go back to verse 8. We are told to have *"compassion one of another,"* or sympathy. The phrase *"love as brethren"* is from the original Greek word that gives us the name Philadelphia, "the city of brotherly love." The final admonition of this verse, *"be pitiful, be courteous,"* is another reference to compassion.

All of these are traits to be found in a righteous life. In I Peter 2:24, when referring to Christ on the cross, Peter encourages us *"that we, being dead to sins, should live unto righteousness."* Our motivation should be to get our minds not just on ourselves, but on others.

Consider the **MEANS**. Verse 9 says, *"Not rendering evil for evil, or railing for railing: but contrariwise blessing; knowing that ye are thereunto called, that ye should inherit a blessing."* The emphasis here is not on the negative but on the positive, which is the blessing.

Many years ago I was preaching in a Bible conference near Albany, New York. While coming up the stairs from the evening meal I helped an elderly man who seemed to be having trouble getting up. I started up a conversation with the gentleman.

"Is your wife here tonight?" I asked.

"No, she is in Heaven."

"I'm sorry."

"Why are you sorry?" he asked. "She is in Heaven."

I asked if any of his children were there with him and he said that all of them were in Heaven as well. Once again I made the mistake of saying I was sorry, and he asked me why I was sorry.

In an attempt to salvage the conversation, I asked if he had any living relatives. He said all of them were in Heaven. That time I was smart enough to say nothing.

"You know, this church is my family," said the man, who was well into his eighties. "I do everything I can to help bring people to Jesus Christ."

That is significance.

When I was in Mexico preaching at a Bible conference I began talking to a young man who was in the Bible College there. He didn't know who I was. I asked him what he was doing there, and he said he was studying to be a pastor.

"Great," I said. "When were you saved?"

He told me about his salvation experience and said it took place in Chambersburg, Pennsylvania, where I was a pastor for many years.

"What church was it?"

"The Open Door Church."

"Who was the pastor?"

"Dino Pedrone."

I told him who he was talking to and he said, "Oh, I didn't know it was you."

Even though I didn't remember that young man and knew nothing about him, a sudden feeling of great significance swept over me because my church had a part in his salvation. The blessing of God comes upon us when we have significance, and I have found the happiest people to be those who enjoy life by serving the Lord.

There is significance in helping others, as illustrated in Proverbs 3:27-28. *"Withhold not good from them to whom it is due, when it is in the power of YOUR hand to do it. Say not unto thy neighbor, Go, and come again, and tomorrow I will give; when thou hast it by thee."*

This is the blessing and privilege of helping others when we have the ability to do so. We can often miss out of the blessing God has for us because we want to hold onto something that we could be using to bless someone else.

There is a great book titled "The Blessing" by Gary Smalley and John Trent. I have read it several times and shared it with others as well. In this book there is a fivefold blessing that pertained to the Old Testament Jewish family.

The first blessing is a meaningful touch. When you go up to a loved one for a hug or similar show of affection, there is something special about that. It is important to have someone we care about close by at certain times.

Look at Genesis 48:9-10 which shows Jacob blessing Joseph's sons. *"And Joseph said unto his father, they are my sons, whom God hath given me in this place. And he said, bring them, I pray thee, unto me, and I will bless them. Now the eyes of Israel were dim for age, so that he could not see. And he brought them near unto him; and he kissed them, and embraced them."*

The words of Jesus about this very thing are found in Mark 10:13-16. *"And they brought young children to him, that he should touch them: and his disciples rebuked those that brought them. But when Jesus saw it, he was much displeased, and said unto them, suffer the little children to come unto me, and forbid them not: for of such is the kingdom of God. Verily I say unto you, whosoever shall not receive the kingdom of God as a little child, he shall not enter therein. And he took them up in his arms, put his hands upon them, and blessed them."*

When I am visiting a church or just going out in public, I often see younger couples holding hands but many times I enjoy seeing older couples doing the same thing. That is a beautiful sight to behold.

In Mark 1:40-42 Jesus did something that no one is ever supposed to do. *"And there came a leper to him, beseeching him, and kneeling down to him, and saying unto him, If thou wilt, thou canst make me clean. And Jesus, moved with compassion, put forth his hand, and touched him, and said unto him, I will; be thou clean. And as soon as he had spoken, immediately the leprosy departed from him, and he was cleansed."* How important a meaningful touch can be to someone.

The second blessing is a spoken word. Proverbs 18:21 says, *"Death and life are in the power of the tongue."* What we say often stays with us for a long time.

I participated in several sports in high school. I played two years on a volleyball team; the first year we were terrible, but the second year we were pretty good. The coach during our first year regularly told us everything we were doing wrong; we already knew what we doing wrong because it was pretty obvious. Once he put me into a game to serve and said, "Whatever you do, don't hit the ball into the net." I actually hit it under the net. He put just enough of a thought in my mind to discourage me.

Our coach the next year told us often how good we were playing, and it was very uplifting for us. The right kind of word, especially when someone is suffering, can help him get through the day.

The third blessing comes in attaching high value to the one who is blessed. Look at Deuteronomy 33:1-2, "*And this is the blessing, wherewith Moses the man of God blessed the children of Israel before his death. And he said, The LORD came from Sinai, and rose up from Seir unto them; he shined forth from mount Paran, and he came with ten thousands of saints: from his right hand went a fiery law for them.*"

Moses knew he would not be going into the Promised Land but would be buried at Mount Nebo. He spent the rest of Deuteronomy 33 giving a blessing to the various tribes of Israel. It was common at this time for a patriarch to do such a thing for his descendants, as we saw Jacob doing earlier. We should try to bless others throughout our lives as we serve the Lord.

When I was a pastor, for many years I would go to my office every single week and find an envelope under my door. It contained a beautiful letter from someone in the church telling me how great the service was. I didn't know who did this. One week I got a glimpse of someone sliding it under the door and I raced over to see who it was, but they vanished like a ghost and were gone. It was years later before I found out who wrote all of those letters – a young single girl who loved the Lord and hardly ever said anything to me in person. But her letters spoke volumes.

It is vital for us to let the people in our lives know how valuable they are to us and how much we appreciate them.

The fourth blessing is a picture of a blessed future. We have many fine young people at Davis College and I remind them frequently that they have a great future. Some of them may not be doing well in school or even entertain thoughts of quitting, but I tell them that God has a great future for them. If we tell them often enough and for long enough, they will get it. I know it took me a while to get it.

When I went to Bible college after high school, I didn't really know why I was there. I had actually signed up for several other colleges before that but had no real interest in any of them. Most high school students are the same way today. We need to make sure we don't tear them down or ridicule them for that. God has a bright future for them as well.

The fifth blessing comes in actively committing to the task that God has for you. I talked recently to a longtime friend of mine named Gary Patton, and he told me something I had never known. In all the years he and his sister were in our Christian school, a men's Bible class took up a weekly offering to pay for their school bills. That is an active commitment to the task.

Do you want to *"love life, and see good days"*? You might say, "Yes, I do. I want more money, a bigger house and a nice car." There is nothing wrong with having those things, but that is not the bottom line when it comes to what I Peter 3 is talking about. Verse 9 says, *"that ye should inherit a blessing."* I believe wholeheartedly that what goes around comes around, and you will reap what you sow. Strive to bless others, and the Bible teaches that you will be blessed as a result.

Consider the **MINISTRY** of peace. This is something we do not hear very much about. Some Christians act as if they believe they are called to start war all the time. There are times when war is necessary to have peace, but that is not always the case.

Look at verse 11. *"Let him eschew evil, and do good; let him seek peace, and ensue it."* The word *"seek"* in this instance means to literally chase after it. It is actually a legal term that implies the idea of a lawsuit, which is adversarial in nature. In essence, we should sue for peace.

I pointed out earlier that I Peter 1:6-7 are the key verses for the entire book. *"Wherein ye greatly rejoice, though now for a season, if need be, ye are in heaviness through manifold temptations: That the trial of your faith, being much more precious than of gold that perisheth, though it be tried with fire, might be found unto praise and honor and glory at the appearing of Jesus Christ."* This is a reminder that we all will go through some trials in life, but that is what tests us, strengthens us and helps us become what God would have us be.

Verses 13-16 of chapter 1 tell us, *"Wherefore gird up the loins of your mind, be sober, and hope to the end for the grace that is to be brought unto you at the revelation of Jesus Christ; As obedient children, not fashioning yourselves according to the former lusts in your ignorance: But as he which hath called you is holy, so be ye holy in all manner of conversation; Because it is written, Be ye holy; for I am holy."*

And we must not forget the words of I Peter 2:9. *"But ye are a chosen generation, a royal priesthood, an holy nation, a peculiar people; that ye should show forth the praises of him who hath called you out of darkness into his marvellous light."*

God is saying through all of these passages, "This is what I have done for you," and that message leads up to what He has to say about suffering. This is not something we want to talk about or think about, but suffering has a way of finding us and capturing us. The Lord wants us to avoid focusing constantly on our suffering but remember our special place in His kingdom as believers and the other things He has mentioned in these verses in I Peter.

The words of Peter in the text we are studying now were already familiar to many when he wrote them, as they are also contained in the Old Testament. Look at Psalms 34:12-16. *"What man is he that desireth life, and loveth many days, that he may see good? Keep thy tongue from evil, and thy lips from speaking guile. Depart from evil, and do good; seek peace, and pursue it. The eyes of the LORD are upon the righteous, and his ears are open unto their cry. The face of the LORD is against them that do evil, to cut off the remembrance of them from the earth."*

There are times in life when we have done all we can do and must simply say, "God, it is yours. I'm turning it completely over to you." It could be a relationship, a health issue or anything else. Psalms 37:5 says, *"Commit thy way unto the LORD; trust also in him; and he shall bring it to pass."* The Hebrew word in that verse for *"commit"* means to just roll it over to God.

I read recently the wonderful story of Jim Cymbala, the pastor of the Brooklyn Tabernacle, whose daughter strayed away from God. It was a great burden to him. At one of the prayer meetings at the church, a group of women came and prayed at the altar.

"Pastor, we are going to pray for you," they said. "We are going to pray that your daughter comes home, and we will claim that from God."

Cymbala had reached a place in his life where he could do nothing else and had given it over to God. As he recounts in his book, "Fresh Wind, Fresh Fire," he was coming down the stairs to the living room and his daughter was standing there waiting for him. She had come home.

One of the things we must remember is that we have an awesome Heavenly Father. The reason we can have a good life and pursue peace is because of Him.

Billy Graham's daughter said once that she came home after wandering in sin for years. "I was driving up the driveway wondering how Dad would respond," she said. "When I arrived, I saw him come out of the house. He put his arms around me, hugged me and said, 'Welcome home.'"

That is how our Heavenly Father is, and that is why we should be pursuing peace.

As we look at I Peter 3:12, consider the MEMORIES. "*For the eyes of the Lord are over the righteous, and his ears are open unto their prayers: but the face of the Lord is against them that do evil.*" God is always pleased with a righteous life.

Psalms 33:5 says, "*He loveth righteousness and judgment: the earth is full of the goodness of the LORD.*" These thoughts are throughout the Word of God:

"*Thou lovest righteousness, and hatest wickedness: therefore God, thy God, hath anointed thee with the oil of gladness above thy fellows*" (Ps. 45:7).

"*The LORD openeth the eyes of the blind: the LORD raiseth them that are bowed down: the LORD loveth the righteous*" (Ps. 146:8).

"*The sacrifice of the wicked is an abomination to the LORD: but the prayer of the upright is his delight*" (Prov. 15:8).

There are so many verses like this. We have a God that wants to hear us and answer us.

In I Peter 3, we see more written about suffering as we get into verse 13 and beyond. Much of that involves suffering for the Lord's sake. But that does not change the fact that He wants us to love life and enjoy it.

I was speaking with a good friend named Art Lawson, a wonderful man of God. A few years ago he went to the hospital for what he thought was a basic procedure and wound up having eight surgeries and plenty of complications. His medical issues delayed some of his ministry work in Scotland and other countries and forced him to stay home for a while.

As we talked, he listed the various things that were going on and quickly added, "But you know it's going to be okay."

How can he say that? It is only possible when you have a Lord like we have.

When my father died he was my best friend. I thought at the time, "He is the best man I know. I can't go on." I went to the funeral home and put my hand on his hand as he lay in the casket. As I did that, the first thing that came to mind was God saying to me, "That's not your dad. He is with Me." From that moment on, I had a peace that passes all understanding.

We need preaching today because we must be reminded in times of despair that Christ and His Word are all we need. So often we suffer, go through heartache and difficulty that seem to overwhelm us, but we can love life and see good days. This is not based on all of the things the world tells us we need to be happy, but on our relationship and walk with God.

We are reaching a challenging point in our study. Suffering is a part of life. Can you love life and see good days during that time? Peter tells us that if our minds are right, we can. It is all possible because we serve an awesome God.

Questions:
1. What are four things we should consider in order to love life and see good days?
2. What is the fivefold blessing that pertained to the Jewish family (Trent/Smalley's book)?

Discussion:
1. What are some of the hindrances you experience when trying to love life and see good days?
2. How can you correct these hindrances?

Chapter 8

SUFFERING FOR RIGHTEOUSNESS' SAKE
I Peter 3:13-4:6

"And who is he who will harm you if you become followers of what is good? But even if you should suffer for righteousness' sake, you are blessed. "And do not be afraid of their threats, nor be troubled. But sanctify the Lord God in your hearts, and always be ready to give a defense to everyone who asks you a reason for the hope that is in you, with meekness and fear; having a good conscience, that when they defame you as evildoers, those who revile your good conduct in Christ may be ashamed. For it is better, if it is the will of God, to suffer for doing good than for doing evil. For Christ also suffered once for sins, the just for the unjust, that He might bring us to God, being put to death in the flesh but made alive by the Spirit, by whom also He went and preached to the spirits in prison,[0] who formerly were disobedient, when once the Divine longsuffering waited in the days of Noah, while the ark was being prepared, in which a few, that is, eight souls, were saved through water.[1] There is also an antitype which now saves us—baptism (not the removal of the filth of the flesh, but the answer of a good conscience toward God), through the resurrection of Jesus Christ,[2] who has gone into heaven and is at the right hand of God, angels and authorities and powers having been made subject to Him. Therefore, since Christ suffered

for us in the flesh, arm yourselves also with the same mind, for he who has suffered in the flesh has ceased from sin,[2] that he no longer should live the rest of his time in the flesh for the lusts of men, but for the will of God.[3] For we have spent enough of our past lifetime in doing the will of the Gentiles—when we walked in lewdness, lusts, drunkenness, revelries, drinking parties, and abominable idolatries. In regard to these, they think it strange that you do not run with them in the same flood of dissipation, speaking evil of you. They will give an account to Him who is ready to judge the living and the dead. For this reason the gospel was preached also to those who are dead, that they might be judged according to men in the flesh, but live according to God in the spirit." **(I Peter 3:13-4:6)**

*I*n the 1940s there were two evangelists in the United States who many people thought were going to be greatly used of God. One was Billy Graham and the other was Charles Templeton.

In Harrisburg, Pennsylvania, Templeton held a crusade that is probably to this day the most effective ever conducted in that city. God greatly used him there. Templeton knew Graham fairly well and they had a conversation that is documented in Templeton's book "Farewell to God."

Templeton, in essence, told Graham, "Billy, if you keep going the way you're going, no one will ever know who you are. You need to go off to the university, study and learn some new things."

Graham thought about this and went out one day into the woods to pray. He decided then that he would continue preaching the gospel.

Templeton went in another direction. As far as his salvation, only eternity will tell for certain, but he began to champion the idea that intellect was more important than anything and righteousness mattered little. He wrote "Farewell to God" near the end of his life.

About that time, during an interview with Lee Strobel, Templeton was asked, "At this point in your life, what do you think of Jesus?" According to Strobel, Templeton wiped a tear from his eye and said, "I miss Him. I really miss Him."

It's one thing to miss a material possession that you once owned or even a loved one who is no longer with us. But it is something else entirely to miss the Son of God, especially when you know the truth.

In the passage from I Peter we are looking at, God is talking not just about salvation but about righteousness and how to live a righteous life for Him. The final words of I Pet. 2:23 refer to Christ as *"him that judgeth righteously"* and the next verse notes that by His death we *"should live unto righteousness."* He was the ultimate example of righteousness for us.

Notice I Peter 3:14, which says, *"But and if ye suffer for righteousness' sake, happy are ye."* This passage is talking about suffering, but not physical suffering. It is when evil is spoken of as good, and good is spoken of as evil. Verses 13-17 show us the **EXPECTATION OF SUFFERING**. If you live for Jesus Christ, you can expect suffering in your life.

Verse 13 gives us an idea of the attitude we need to have. *"And who is he that will harm you, if ye be followers of that which is good?"* The word *"good"* here is from the Greek word *agathos*. It speaks of God's favor.

But the next verse, as we have seen, tells us that if we suffer for righteousness' sake we are blessed. That verse is actually a quote from the book of Isaiah.

The last part of verse 14 says, *"be not afraid of their terror, neither be troubled."* Our attitude should be that no matter what happens, God loves us and will protect us.

The apologetic is given in verse 15. *"But sanctify the Lord God in your hearts: and be ready always to give an answer to every man that asketh you a reason of the hope that is in you with meekness and fear."*

Do you know what you believe? If someone asks you what you believe, can you give that person an answer? Can you defend it intellectually as well as spiritually?

We are living in Biblical illiteracy. When I first went to Practical Bible Training School, even though I was reared in a good home and a good church, I did not know the Bible. I learned about the Bible in at the Bible school.

I am so encouraged when I speak in a conference and see the congregation filled with people who have their Bibles in front of them and their notebooks open so they can write down what they hear. These are people who want to know the Word of God, and there needs to be a new thirst in America for that knowledge.

I tell some students to come to Davis College for one year and get a solid Biblical foundation and worldview, regardless of whether they choose to stay beyond that. We have young people coming out of good Christian homes and good churches who go off to college and don't even go to church anymore. One of the reasons for that is because they simply do not know what they believe. We as Christians need to be able to defend what we believe.

There is also an expectation of suffering because of our answer. Look at verses 16-17. *"Having a good conscience; that, whereas they speak evil of you, as of evildoers, they may be ashamed that falsely accuse your good conversation in Christ. For it is better, if the will of God be so, that ye suffer for well doing, than for evil doing."*

Verse 16 says that people will try to defame us because of our faith, but our answers in good conscience will confound them.

As I studied these passages I began to recall a five-minute daily radio program called "Guidelines" that I conducted many years ago in Pennsylvania. I went to a local radio station to record them, and I would usually do an entire week of programs at one time so I would not have to go to the station every day.

When I recorded these broadcasts, a man sat behind the glass working as the producer and engineer (he was often the only person at the station at that time). As I spoke during the broadcast, he would listen and look at me intently, sometimes even making faces at me. Occasionally he laughed or slapped his forehead as if to say, "I can't believe what you're saying!"

I told my wife, "I don't know if anyone is listening to that radio program, but I'm just going to keep preaching right to him."

So I started getting into it and enjoying it even more. I talked and he laughed, and when I left he would say, "I can't believe you're saying those things on the air."

"Just wait until next week," I replied.

We became good friends as a result of this. His name was Al. One day he called me on the phone and said, "I want you to come to my apartment."

I thought he wanted to debate, and I put him off for a while. Finally I went to his place, which was a two-room apartment above a store and coffee bar. We met in the coffee bar and he didn't say much at first. We went up to his room, then back down and back up again. I asked him what he wanted.

"You really believe what you say you believe, don't you?" he asked.

"Yes, I do," I replied.

"My life has been so empty. I want to learn more about this."

I was astounded that he said that. That night I led him to Christ, and within one year he was an engineer on a television program for a national Christian broadcaster. All those times he ridiculed me for what I was saying, he knew he didn't have any answers for his own life. Thank God that he was able to learn those answers through His Word.

We find the **EXAMPLE OF SUFFERING** in verses 18-22. If you live righteously for Jesus Christ, there will be heartache and difficulty that come our way. The greatest example of this is given by Christ Himself, through His atonement for our sins.

Verse 18 says, "*For Christ also hath once suffered for sins, the just for the unjust, that he might bring us to God, being put to death in the flesh, but quickened by the Spirit.*"

Notice the word "*once.*" Jesus is not continually suffering for us. He did it one time. We are asked when we observe the Lord's Table in our churches to do it "*in remembrance of*" what Christ did for us that one time.

Look at I John 2:1-2. "*My little children, these things write I unto you, that ye sin not. And if any man sin, we have an advocate with the Father, Jesus Christ the righteous: And he is the propitiation for our sins: and not for ours only, but also for the sins of the whole world.*" Jesus took care of it all at once.

We read in Hebrews 9:25-26, "*Nor yet that he should offer himself often, as the high priest entereth into the holy place every year with blood of others; For then must he often have suffered since the foundation of the world: but now once in the end of the world hath he appeared to put away sin by the sacrifice of himself."*

The point is emphasized again in Hebrews 10:12. *"But this man, after he had offered one sacrifice for sins for ever, sat down on the right hand of God."* Christ only had to die once.

The result of that sacrifice is seen in Hebrews 10:17-18. *"And their sins and iniquities will I remember no more. Now where remission of these is, there is no more offering for sin."* Aren't you glad about that? The ultimate example of suffering is Christ and His atonement for us.

We saw in I Peter 3:18 that Christ died physically, but was made alive by the Spirit and never died spiritually. That thought is continued in verse 19: *"By which also he went and preached unto the spirits in prison."* This refers to the time between Christ's death and the resurrection, when He went to what He called Paradise and the Old Testament saints were released to go to Heaven with Him.

It is also referenced in Ephesians 4:8-10. *"Wherefore he saith, When he ascended up on high, he led captivity captive, and gave gifts unto men. (Now that he ascended, what is it but that he also descended first into the lower parts of the earth? He that descended is the same also that ascended up far above all heavens, that he might fill all things.)"*

Another reference is found in I Peter 4:6. *"For this cause was the gospel preached also to them that are dead, that they might be judged according to men in the flesh, but live according to God in the spirit."* What Christ did in going to the cross is an overwhelming thing, but what He did after His death and prior to His resurrection is what gives us such hope and assurance for eternal life.

Look at I Peter 3:20. *"Which sometime were disobedient, when once the longsuffering of God waited in the days of Noah, while the ark was a preparing, wherein few, that is, eight souls were saved by water."* This verse illustrates the grace of God in going to such lengths to save only eight people out of the entire world during Noah's life.

Verse 21 says, *"The like figure whereunto even baptism doth also now save us (not the putting away of the filth of the flesh, but the answer of a good conscience toward God,) by the resurrection of*

Jesus Christ." This is also called an "*antitype*" in some translations. Baptism does not save us, but it is a picture of our obedience to God and our desire to walk in newness of life. One of the great thrills for a church is to see new converts follow the Lord in believer's baptism.

As we see in verse 22, Jesus "*is gone into heaven, and is on the right hand of God; angels and authorities and powers being made subject unto him.*"

These verses contain the heart of the Gospel message. Jesus died on the cross, was buried, rose again, set the captives free, and now sits on the right hand of God to intercede for you and me.

I have learned something in my life when I lead people to Christ. Some of them wanted nothing to do with God a moment before, but suddenly you look at them and you see that something has changed. That is the work of the Holy Spirit. A lot of people out there are claiming that there are many ways to God and to Heaven, but that is not true. What Jesus did 2,000 years ago is still changing lives today, and if we have to suffer for righteousness' sake it is worth it.

The first six verses of I Peter 4 show us the **EXPERIENCE OF SUFFERING**. Verses 1-2 give us a present lesson. "*Forasmuch then as Christ hath suffered for us in the flesh, arm yourselves likewise with the same mind: for he that hath suffered in the flesh hath ceased from sin; That he no longer should live the rest of his time in the flesh to the lusts of men, but to the will of God.*"

I believe that there are times in our lives when we should stop and meditate about the cross and what Christ did for us. Our former church in Florida sponsored numerous showings of the film "The Passion of the Christ" in local theaters and we saw many come to Christ. Some people said the depiction of Jesus in that film showed too much suffering and it probably was too much for human eyes in some places, but I don't think it begins to describe the suffering our Lord went through.

When you think of our Savior – who could have simply spoken and summoned legions of angels to His side – going to the cross after being beaten as He was, it is almost too much to comprehend. As Isaiah 52:4 put it, "*his visage was so marred more than any man, and his form more than the sons of men.*" The sins of the world

– past, present and future – were placed upon Him. The physical agony was overwhelming, but when He cried out, "*It is finished*," it was done once and for all.

I visited a jail once to see a man who said he needed the Lord. Wanting to help him as much as I could, I asked him why he was incarcerated. He told a story of multiplied molestations of children that turned my stomach. I went through the plan of salvation thinking to myself, "This man shouldn't be saved," and I even asked him if he knew for sure what he was doing. It was as if the Holy Spirit had to convict me to lead him to Christ.

But the same Jesus that will save a man like that is the One we need to stand for. He will save that man just as quickly as He saves me or you. When you think about what you should say or do to defend your faith, go back in your mind to the image of Christ on the cross and remember what He did for you. As you pray, imagine that you are walking into the very throne room of God, and remember that Jesus died for sinners just like us.

Notice in verses 3-4 the past life. "*For the time past of our life may suffice us to have wrought the will of the Gentiles, when we walked in lasciviousness, lusts, excess of wine, revellings, banquetings, and abominable idolatries: Wherein they think it strange that ye run not with them to the same excess of riot, speaking evil of you.*"

Often when a person comes to Christ it leads to ridicule and anger from his so-called friends. People will go to great lengths to keep you from living righteously. Let me challenge you right now to stand for Jesus no matter what. With so many being martyred around the world for their faith, and the constant pull of those who would convince us of a false religion or that there are many ways to God, we need more than ever to stand firm for Him.

Look at verses 5-6. "*Who shall give account to him that is ready to judge the quick and the dead. For this cause was the gospel preached also to them that are dead, that they might be judged according to men in the flesh, but live according to God in the spirit.*" Here we have the future life. The Gospel must go forward, and we need to speak boldly about Jesus and what He has done in our lives.

Winston Churchill has given many great speeches, and I have recordings of some of them at home that I love to listen to. Perhaps his most famous speech was at the low point of World War II, when he gave a commencement address at a Harrow prep school. These were some of his words:

"Never give in. Never give in. Never, never, never, in nothing small, large or petty; never give in except to convictions of honor and good sense. Never give in."

It probably is the most famous address he ever gave because of his challenge that England would never give up the fight.

This world is just a starting point and we are only here for a brief period of time. While we are here, let's make it clear that we are followers of our Lord and Savior, Jesus Christ.

Questions:
1. How is Jesus the greatest example of suffering?
2. What illustration does Peter use as an antitype in this chapter?

Discussion:
1. What are some examples of times you have experienced suffering for the gospel's sake?

Chapter 9

BE AWARE THAT JESUS IS COMING!
I Peter 4:7-19

"But the end of all things is at hand: be ye therefore sober, and watch unto prayer. And above all things have fervent charity among yourselves: for charity shall cover the multitude of sins. Use hospitality one to another without grudging. As every man hath received the gift, even so minister the same one to another, as good stewards of the manifold grace of God. If any man speak, let him speak as the oracles of God; if any man minister, let him do it as of the ability which God giveth: that God in all things may be glorified through Jesus Christ, to whom be praise and dominion fo ever and ever. Amen. Beloved, think it not strange concerning the fiery trial which is to try you, as though some strange thing happened unto you: but rejoice, inasmuch as ye are partakers of Christ's sufferings; that, when his glory shall be revealed, ye may be glad also with exceeding joy. If ye be reproached for the name of Christ, happy are ye; for the spirit of glory and of God resteth upon you: on their part he is evil spoken of, but on your part he is glorified. But let none of you suffer as a murderer, or as a thief, or as an evildoer, or as a busybody in other men's matters. Yet if any man suffer as a Christian, let him not be ashamed; but let him glorify God on this behalf. For the time is come that judgment must begin at the house of God: and if

it first begin at us, what shall the end be of them that obey not the gospel of God? And if the righteous scarcely be saved, where shall the ungodly and the sinner appear? Wherefore let them that suffer according to the will of God commit the keeping of their souls to him in well doing, as unto a faithful Creator." **(I Peter 4:7-19)**

*I*n chapter 2 of this book, our attention was on one verse in I Peter about the coming of Christ and then there was a perusal of I & II Peter addressing the many verses about the Messiah's return. On one of my visits to Israel, I and our group met with Chief Rabbi Yona Mentzer. In his remarks to our group he said "When Messiah comes we will ask him the question, were you here before?" "That," he said, "is the difference between us and the evangelists." The chief rabbi used the word evangelists and we would say evangelicals. The rabbi has a point. The difference, of course, is huge.

Christians in Peter's day joined the apostle expecting the imminent return of our Lord. There are many excellent Bible scholars and teachers who believe Christ is coming but they view it differently. I personally believe Christ can come at any time in what has historically been referred to as the rapture. The fact is Jesus is coming. Later in the II epistle of Peter the apostle states, *"The Lord is not slack concerning his promise, as some men count slackness; but is longsuffering to us-ward, not willing that any should perish, but that all should come to repentance."* (II Peter 3:9). The Lord is bringing people into His family. One day He will come. It matters not about what day He will come, we know that we will see Him. In this passage Peter gives a number of things we ought to be aware of in light of the coming of our Lord. He reminds the readers to be sober (4:7), watch and to pray (4:9), rejoice (4:13) and to glorify God (4:6-19).

The Idea of being sober is important. There are fanatics who talk about wild concepts concerning our Lord's return. They pump people into a frenzy only to 'let the air' out of their prophetical balloon when their predictions go awry. We need to be careful of the wild and the bizarre. Date setting, sign sharing, and stiff warnings must always be compared with the sober minded in Scripture. We are to be sober minded. It means to be careful about tangents. The term means "to have a steady mind".

We need to live knowing that Jesus Christ may come today.

Peter mentions "The end of all things is at hand." He is not telling us to "give up" and sit idly by. He is telling us to get ready.

Two thousand years have passed and our Lord has not come. God the Father knows the day and hour our blessed Lord will return.

In this section he addresses our lifestyle in several areas in light of the coming of Christ. He talks about our relationship to the saints (4:8-11), expectancy of suffering (4:12-14), and our examination of personal living (4:15-19).

Relationship with Saints

History records numerous Christians who have suffered persecution. The early church at Jerusalem had its greatest growth through persecution. The Christian life is counterproductive to the worlds. The world lives with an entitlement mentality. A Christian is to live with a servant's mentality. In Genesis we find the genesis of a spiritual warfare between Satan and God. Genesis 3:15 says, *"And I will put enmity between thee and the woman, and between thy seed and her seed; it shall bruise thy head, and thou shalt bruise his heel."* A believer is to glorify God. The enemy does not want to glorify God. Christians should not be surprised when there is persecution. Jesus said, *"In the world you shall have tribulation: but be of good cheer: I have overcome the world"* (John 16:33). I Peter 4:11 addresses the importance of proclaiming truth. The truth is spoken of as the oracle of God. When God's oracles go forth some will believe, others will be neutral, others will be offended and stand against the truth.

Expectancy of Suffering – I Peter 4:12-14

The term "fire" is a term that refers to difficulties, persecutions, tribulation, and tests in life. This text refers to the trouble that comes because we are faithful to God. The word trial is from a Greek word that speaks of "things going together."

Peter states that we are to understand we are to rejoice in suffering. Philippians 3:10 records, *"That I may know him, and the power of his resurrection, and the fellowship of his sufferings, being*

made conformable unto his death". Fellowship refers to commu-
nion. When we suffer for Christ because of doing the right thing we
are drawn closer to Him.

It is my opinion that the Western Hemisphere is Laodicean in
nature in that we are doing and living "people's rights." The church of
Laodicea is the last church that is addressed in the book of Revelation
(Rev. 3:14-23) and it is the lukewarm church that demands people's
rights. We need to be careful to follow the Scriptures and not the
rights of humans.

The world talks about the absence of persecution as a good
thing. The trial of our faith is the assurance of glory based on
the truth of our Lord's return. Discipline leads to the glory of an
accomplishment. It is true of the artist, musician, or athlete. If you
are facing trouble remember our Lord is using this for His glory
and your good.

In verse 13, Peter reminds followers of Christ, *"Be constantly
rejoicing. . ."* Some translate it simply "but rejoice". Four times in
the verses he mentions joy. The joy is based on the privilege we
have. One privilege is our relationship with Christ is enhanced, for
as we suffer we further identify with Jesus. In verse 14 it brings us
to a closer walk with the Holy Spirit. This reference is a reminder of
the Shekinah glory that dwelt in the Old Testament. Both the taber-
nacle and the temple were under the cloud of the Shekinah glory. It
was a reminder of the presence of God. Exodus 40:34 reminds us of
the presence of God, *"Then a cloud covered the tent of the congre-
gation, and the glory of the Lord filled the tabernacle"*. Again, in I
Kings 8:10, *"And it came to pass, when the priests were come out
of the holy place, that the cloud filled the house of the Lord, so that
the priests could not stand to minister because of the cloud: for the
glory of the Lord had filled the house of the Lord."*

Back in the beginning of our study in I Peter the apostle talked
about *"joy unspeakable and full of glory"* (I Peter 1:7-8). The book
of Philippians was penned by the apostle Paul when he was in prison
and the theme of the book is Joy. His admonition is *"Rejoice in the
Lord always. Again I will say rejoice"* (Philippians 4:4).

It is amazing to me how history reveals individuals who sang
praises to God and glorified Him when going through deep persecu-

tion. Paul and Silas sang hymns when they were in jail (Acts 16). The glory of the future was in their lives.

Authority is found in Christ. The devil despises the very name of Jesus. When we stand for Christ we exalt the name that many reproach. The name Christian was a name held in contempt in the early days of Christianity, Christians were also called people of "The Way," which referred to people following Christ as The Way. When Saul of Tarsus started on his trip on the Damascus Road he was looking for people of The Way (Acts 9:2) to persecute and bring them as prisoners to Jerusalem. Little did he know that he would shortly be a member of "The Way" (Acts 9:20).

Examining our Personal Life – I Peter 4: 15-18

The fiery trial can be a time of growth. It is as some commentators call it the refining fire. God is refining, purifying, and building our lives for His kingdom. Peter reminds us that he is not speaking of one who is an evildoer. Perhaps he remembers his own failure prior to Jesus death on the cross. He failed when he denied the Lord but shortly his life was changed. We who are members of the household of God need to identify with our Lord's suffering. Keep short sin accounts. Quickly confess sin. Ultimately the world wants to see Jesus in our lives. They need the wonderful Savior. Verse 19 is a challenge to commitment. The word *"commit"* is a banking term. It is speaking of depositing. God has redeemed, sanctified and glorified His people. The term here speaks of constant commitment.

Note in closing this chapter that Peter speaks of a faithful Creator. God takes care of those who are His. As Creator, He is over all things. God is our Father, our Creator, and our Sustainer. Whatever you may be going through, remember above all to look to Him for your source of strength.

Questions:
1. The word "commit" is a _____ term. It speaks of _____.
2. The term "fire" is a term that refers to _____.
3. The tabernacle and the temple of the Old Testament were under a cloud. What is the name of the cloud?

Discussion:

    1. Think through a recent fiery trial you experienced in your life. How did you get through it?

Chapter 10

A FAITHFUL CREATOR
I Peter 4:19 – 5:14

"Wherefore let them that suffer according to the will of God commit the keeping of their souls to him in well doing, as unto a faithful Creator. The elders which are among you I exhort, who am also an elder, and a witness of the sufferings of Christ, and also a partaker of the glory that shall be revealed: feed the flock of God which is among you, taking the oversight thereof, not by constraint, but willingly; not for filthy lucre, but of a ready mind; neither as being lords over God's heritage, but being examples to the flock. And when the chief Shepherd shall appear, ye shall receive a crown of glory that fadeth not away. Likewise, ye younger, submit yourselves unto the elder. Yea, all of you be subject one to another, and be clothed with humility: for God resisteth the proud, and giveth grace to the humble. Humble yourselves therefore under the mighty hand of God, that he may exalt you in due time: casting all your care upon him; for he careth for you. Be sober, be vigilant; because your adversary the devil, as a roaring lion, walketh about, seeking whom he may devour: Whom resist stedfast in the faith, knowing that the same afflictions are accomplished in your brethren that are in the world. But the God of all grace, who hath called us unto his eternal glory by Christ Jesus, after that ye have suffered a while, make you perfect, stablish, strengthen, settle you. To him be glory and dominion for ever and ever. Amen. By Silvanus, a faithful brother

unto you, as I suppose, I have written briefly, exhorting, and testifying that this is the true grace of God wherein ye stand. The church that is at Babylon, elected together with you, saluteth you; and so doth Marcus my son. Greet ye one another with a kiss of charity. Peace be with you all that are in Christ Jesus. Amen." (**I Peter 4:19 – 5:14**)

*I*t is commonly accepted that the chapter and verse divisions in the Bible were determined after the canon of Scripture was written, and sometimes we find a thought in one chapter that is directly connected to the next chapter as if they were written at the same time.

This is the case in I Peter 4:19, which ends with the words, *"as unto a faithful Creator."* That verse is a perfect segue into I Peter 5, as that phrase is a fitting title for the fifth chapter of I Peter. We have a God who is a faithful Creator.

The idea of a faithful Creator is an appropriate conclusion to I Peter, which began with a theme centering on the goodness of God. All of the instruction in the book of I Peter that would help us live for Him is tied to that theme.

The final chapter of I Peter is actually a message from God, beginning with His challenge to the leaders of the church in verses 1-4. *"The elders which are among you I exhort, who am also an elder, and a witness of the sufferings of Christ, and also a partaker of the glory that shall be revealed: Feed the flock of God which is among you, taking the oversight thereof, not by constraint, but willingly; not for filthy lucre, but of a ready mind; Neither as being lords over God's heritage, but being examples to the flock. And when the chief Shepherd shall appear, ye shall receive a crown of glory that fadeth not away."*

The word *"elders"* in verse 1 of chapter 5 is the Greek word *presbuteros*, one of three terms used interchangeably in the New Testament to describe the pastor or leader of a church. Ephesians 4:11-12 says, *"And he gave some, apostles; and some, prophets; and some, evangelists; and some, pastors and teachers; for the per-*

fecting of the saints, for the work of the ministry, for the edifying of the body of Christ."

A pastor is seen as a shepherd and also as an elder. Look at Titus 1:5-7. *"For this cause left I thee in Crete, that thou shouldest set in order the things that are wanting, and ordain elders in every city, as I had appointed thee: If any be blameless, the husband of one wife, having faithful children not accused of riot or unruly. For a bishop must be blameless, as the steward of God; not selfwilled, not soon angry, not given to wine, no striker, not given to filthy lucre."*

There are several passages that address the office of a pastor. It is one thing to be called to preach, but it is something else to be a pastor.

I believe that there are many men of various ages whom God has called to preach, but we sometimes do not extend the call verbally and publicly to be pastors. In the northeastern United States the number of pastors has gone down dramatically. The reason I left the Sunshine State to come back to my hometown of Binghamton, New York, was because I knew Davis College was training men and women for ministry, and it is in a part of the country that desperately needs preachers.

The importance of having men of God in place in our churches is emphasized in I Peter 5. Verse 2 says that such men should be careful overseers of their congregations and should do so willingly and eagerly, not for financial gain.

On that note, let me say that many churches do not pay their pastors enough. Many pastors come to retirement age and have nothing to retire on, but they keep on preaching because no church has properly taken care of them. On the other side of the coin, there are pastors who will not go to a church unless they are going to receive a certain salary. This puts smaller churches in a bind because they cannot afford someone they feel would be good for their ministry.

A man who is called of God to preach must go into the ministry knowing that God will take care of him. However, each church must realize that the pastor is a gift to them and they should take proper care of the man of God.

When my wife and I went to Chambersburg, Pennsylvania, to assume the pastorate of a church there, we saw tremendous growth.

We went from about 100 people to nearly 1,000 people in three years by the grace of God. It was so exciting to see what the Lord was doing.

A man came to visit me and said he wanted to show me another church. I told him I was not interested in another pastorate, but he showed my wife and me the church and a beautiful home that he would give us (he was a builder) if I became pastor of his church.

It was a very tempting offer. We thought about it a lot, but my wife and I made the decision that no one would ever bring us in by paying too much money or drive us away by paying too little. It has been difficult at times to live by that mantra, but we decided that we were called of God and would have to live that way. That has served us well over the years. Verses 3-4 remind us that when the pastor is the appropriate example to a congregation, God will reward him for that. A crown of glory awaits him!

A message for the learners of the church in contained in verse 5. *"Likewise, ye younger, submit yourselves unto the elder. Yea, all of you be subject one to another, and be clothed with humility: for God resisteth the proud, and gives grace to the humble."*

The idea of submission to elders is a wonderful thought in the Word of God. The elder can be defined as leaders in the church or simply someone who is older. It is important for young people to realize that we as older people love them and want to help them, and we have great empathy for the needs in their lives. This verse is an important reminder from God that they should listen to those who have come along before them and traveled down the same roads they are now traveling.

In the Eastern world there is great respect for those who are older. The Western world places a great deal of emphasis on the young, the athletic and the intellectual, which is the opposite of what the Bible teaches. We all should have the attitude that we are still learning, regardless of our age or station in life.

Verses 6-11 are directed to the laborers of the church. *"Humble yourselves therefore under the mighty hand of God, that he may exalt you in due time: Casting all your care upon him; for he careth for you. Be sober, be vigilant; because your adversary the devil, as a roaring lion, walketh about, seeking whom he may devour:*

Whom resist stedfast in the faith, knowing that the same afflictions are accomplished in your brethren that are in the world. But the God of all grace, who hath called us unto his eternal glory by Christ Jesus, after that ye have suffered a while, make you perfect, stablish, strengthen, settle you. To him be glory and dominion forever and ever. Amen."

This is a message for those who have suffered in their work for the Lord. Verses 6-7 remind us to be influenced by the continual presence of God in our lives and to give Him all of our worries and our burdens. It is so easy to have a high point in a conference or a great meeting with our dear friends and fellow Christians, only to return home and run headlong into a major problem that will put us back into despair. We must always remind ourselves that God cares for us.

Verse 8 is about the battle that we are in. *"Be sober, be vigilant"* means to focus your mind and be wide awake in the face of the adversary. II Timothy 2:26 says, *"And that they may recover themselves out of the snare of the devil, who are taken captive by him at his will."* The devil loves to preoccupy our minds and it causes us to think about things that benefit us very little at the end of the day. We all understand that we will face suffering as children of God, but if the work of God is to go forward it will have to be through the people of God – people like you and me.

Verse 9 challenges us to be strong and firm, putting our faith in God and guarding our minds from that which would harm us. By facing the afflictions of the devil, we are part of a brotherhood of faith that stretches around the world. Somewhere in the world today there has already been a martyr for Jesus Christ. People in other countries are suffering for their faith more than you and I can possibly imagine.

But remember what a great God we serve.

Romans 15:5, says that He is *"the God of patience and consolation."* Romans 15:13 calls Him *"the God of hope."* II Corinthians 13:11 says that He is "the God of love." According to Hebrews 13:20, He is *"the God of peace."* I Peter 1:15 refers to Him as the God of holiness, and in I Peter 5:10 we see that He is *"the God of all grace."*

Verse 10 also reminds us that our foundation and strength is in Him amid our suffering for righteousness' sake, and all glory and honor is attributed to Him in verse 11. The *"amen"* at the end of that verse signifies absolute trust, just as when we say "Amen" in church we are saying that we trust and believe exactly what was said.

The chapter concludes with a few words for the loved of the church in verses 12-14. *"By Silvanus, a faithful brother unto you, as I suppose, I have written briefly, exhorting, and testifying that this is the true grace of God wherein ye stand. The church that is at Babylon, elected together with you, saluteth you; and so doth Marcus my son. Greet ye one another with a kiss of charity. Peace be with you all that are in Christ Jesus. Amen."*

Silvanus was likely the scribe who wrote these words for Peter, and he was acclaimed for his faithfulness. Marcus may have been a biological son.

The final salutation was directed to those who are *"in Christ Jesus."* All of us who are saved are in Christ. This is a common thought throughout the New Testament. In the book of Ephesians the word *"in"* is used 93 times to refer to those who are in Him. However, if we are in Him, there must be those around us and in the world who are not.

The church is a place for the saints of God to come and be fed the Word of God, but that is not all. It is the responsibility of the saints of God to take the message of God to those who need it outside the walls of the church. We need to challenge ourselves anew to be that kind of Christian and reach others for the cause of Christ. If we do not, we are failing in our Christian walk.

I have a friend named Don in north Florida who oversees a Bible institute. He came to Christ at 39 years of age and it was an exciting time for him. He was about to become the president of the local Teamsters union in his area but he decided he would rather give that up and study the Word of God. He eventually earned a doctor of theology degree.

I remember something really special about when Don came to Christ. His father was extremely angry at God and at religion, and he wanted nothing to do with the Gospel. However, Don had a great burden for his dad and twice he made an eight-hour drive just to witness to him. Both times his father told him that if he had come to talk about religion, he should just turn right around and go back home.

One day at our church we had a special Sunday and planned to bring in many unsaved people. During a prayer meeting in my office about an hour before the service began, Don walked in. "My dad is in town and I want you to pray that he will come today," he said.

Don was a truck driver at that time. I will never forget what he said next as he pointed his finger at me.

"If my dad comes today, he will need to hear the Gospel," he said. "You're going to preach the Gospel today, aren't you?"

"Yes," I replied. "I am."

As we prayed that morning, Don wept. He was suffering because his dad was not in Christ. I thought about how wonderful it would be if he came to church that morning.

I was a little late walking out to the church lobby before the service and Don came up to me. "My dad is here," he said. "Go over and say hello to him."

Don's father was standing in a corner of the lobby not talking to anyone. He looked like he was mad at the whole world.

"Sir, I am so glad you are here," I said as I greeted him.

"I'm glad to be here, too," he replied, although I knew that was not a heartfelt sentiment.

He said little else so I walked back toward the auditorium, wondering if he would stay. He came in a little later and sat toward the very back.

I preached a Gospel message as I told Don I would, and many people came forward to receive Christ that morning. As the service was drawing to a close and the choir was just finishing its song of invitation, I looked up and saw Don's father coming down the center aisle, staggering almost like a drunken man, so I went down from the platform to greet him.

"Sir, did you come to be saved?" I asked.

He just looked at me. A tear came down his cheek but he never said anything. I directed one of the counselors at the front to take him aside and show him how to be saved.

Don was on the other side of the auditorium, talking to a couple about the Lord. If you have ever done personal work at the altar in your church, you know that you are never to leave someone just sitting there. But that is what Don did when he saw his dad.

"Oh, Dad," he said, loud enough for 1,500 people in the congregation to hear, as they all walked together over to the side of the auditorium.

His father gave his life to Christ that morning. A few moments later I was reading some of the decision cards to the congregation and I asked him to stand, telling the congregation what I have just written. Many people in our church had been praying for him, and thunderous applause broke out among the congregation at his salvation. It was more exciting than any championship sporting event will ever be.

When I spoke to him after the service he was much calmer than he had been before.

"I am so glad you came to Christ," I told him.

"So am I," he said in a deep voice.

I told him that when I saw him before the service I didn't think he wanted to be there. He assured me I was right.

"Then why did you come?" I asked.

"I wanted to get my son off my back once and for all."

I was so curious about why he decided to accept Christ, so I asked him. He looked me in the eye and said something I will never forget.

"It had nothing to do with your sermon." (Now isn't that encouraging?)

"Then what was it?"

"There was something about the atmosphere in this building."

I thought about that for a moment and then I realized what he was talking about.

Some Christians come to church thinking, "I hope you can bless me, pastor – and do it in 30 minutes because I have things to do." Others come in and they can't get enough.

By the same token, some lost people come to church and think, "These people are nuts. I can't wait to get out of here." Others come to a service and realize, "This is exactly what I have been looking for."

In this case, the difference was the preparation for the service begun by one man who prayed for months that his dad would come to Jesus. I have seen that happen over and over again.

That man has since died and is in Heaven. His son is at peace as he teaches in a Bible institute in Florida, having no worries about whether he will see Dad again.

Lost people come to Christ because we go the extra mile to reach them. If we do not do this, then pray tell who will? We put so much emphasis on what we do at church, but if we do not walk out of our churches and tell people about the Lord, what good is it?

Think about how you react when a visitor walks into a service and sits near you smelling bad or dressed in an odd manner. Perhaps it is a man who everyone knows has been divorced several times and is pursuing a woman in your church. It might just be someone who comes so that his son will leave him alone. How do you feel about people like that?

Maybe the better question is this: How do you feel about your own parent or child who does not know Jesus? The final words of I Peter are ". . .*in Christ Jesus. Amen.*" That should mean something to us.

During 2009, I was the president of Davis College in New York while still serving as pastor of New Testament Baptist Church in Miami, so I was on an airplane every single week of the year. Because I flew so often I was put in the first-class section most of the time. I love the roomy seats and extra service in first class.

I have also found that people in first class are less likely to want to talk about the Lord than those in coach. But one day I met an 18-year-old man who was flying in first class for the first time and did not even know how he got there.

As I witnessed to him, he told me how his parents had gone in different directions and he was living with someone else, among other things in his life. I noticed that he drank alcohol the entire time we talked, so I thought I should witness to him quickly before he became too incoherent.

When I got done telling him the wonderful story of our Lord, he said, "I have never heard anything like that in my entire life. But

I have a grandmother who has prayed for years that would become 'born again.' Is that what you are talking about?"

"Yes, that's about it," I said. "Why don't you become born again right now?"

He prayed and received Christ. I reached for his liquor and suggested we throw it away, and he said that was fine with him. Sometime after that flight, I imagine a grandmother got a phone call from a young university student who said, "Grandma, I'm born again now."

Do you know what the United States of America needs more than anything? It needs God's people, who are called by God's name, to go out and tell the wonderful story of the Savior to those who need Him so desperately. May we become more determined than ever to tell others about Jesus Christ and bring them into the family of God. The faithful creator will be pleased!

Questions:
1. What are the three terms that describe a pastor?
2. God is called the "God of. . ." several times in the chapter. What are some of those terms?
3. Who is Silvanus?

Discussion:
1. When was your last witnessing experience and what happened?

Chapter 11

MAKE SURE OF YOUR CALLING
II Peter 1:1-11

"Simon Peter, a servant and an apostle of Jesus Christ, to them that have obtained like precious faith with us through the righteousness of God and our Savior Jesus Christ: grace and peace be multiplied unto you through the knowledge of God, and of Jesus our Lord, according as his divine power hath given unto us all things that pertain unto life and godliness, through the knowledge of him that hath called us to glory and virtue: whereby are given unto us exceeding great and precious promises: that by these ye might be partakers of the divine nature, having escaped the corruption that is in the world through lust. And beside this, giving all diligence, add to your faith virtue; and to virtue knowledge; and to knowledge temperance; and to temperance patience; and to patience godliness; and to godliness brotherly kindness; and to brotherly kindness charity. For if these things be in you, and abound, they make you that ye shall neither be barren nor unfruitful in the knowledge of our Lord Jesus Christ. But he that lacketh these things is blind, and cannot see afar off, and hath forgotten that he was purged from his old sins. Wherefore the rather, brethren, give diligence to make your calling and election sure: for if ye do these things, ye shall never fall: for so an entrance shall be ministered unto you abundantly into the everlasting kingdom of our Lord and Saviour Jesus Christ." **(II Peter 1:1-11)**

*W*hat exactly is the Christian life? Religion abounds everywhere. Once a person trusts Jesus Christ as their Savior the next step is to grow in grace. So what exactly is this and what does it look like?

The key in II Peter to understand what the Christian life is and what it is not is found in the word know or forms of the word. The term is found at least fourteen times in II Peter. (1:2); (1:3); (1:5); (1:6); (1:8); (1:12); (1:16); (1:20); (2:20); (2:21); (3:3); (3:17); (3:18).

The beginning of II Peter is the Christian life based upon faith.

The Christian Life is a Faith Life – II Peter 1:1-7

Peter opens the book with a typical statement about his servanthood to Christ and his call to apostleship. He then, in verse one, goes into the heart of the issue by calling the Christian life *"like precious faith"*. Peter was with Christ. You and I were not. We, however, have the same calling to salvation as the apostle did (1:10).

Our faith is in a person who is literally the God/man. Verse one speaks of *". . .our God and Savior Jesus Christ."* The word 'and' is the Greek *kai* and can be rendered *"even"*. Our God is a trinity and Jesus is as much God as the Father and Spirit are. Jesus is spoken of here as Savior. Jesus is called Savior several times in this epistle (II Peter 1:11; 2:20; 3:2; 3:18). The idea of a Savior speaks of deliverance. Jesus gave His life on the cross and died for the sins of the world. This is attained because of the "righteousness" of our Savior. He is the all wise, all perfect God. When a sinner trusts Jesus, amazingly His righteousness is then applied to our life. We have a new standing in Him (Titus 3:5).

The apostle goes from righteousness then to the vehicle that is used. The vehicle is the grace of God. Grace as previously mentioned is God's riches at Christ's expense. God is the giver of grace which is undeserved and unmerited. Then from Christ's righteousness we go to grace and the result is the peace of God. Peace with God is stated in Romans 5:1, *"Therefore being justified by faith, we have peace with God through our Lord Jesus Christ"* and the peace of God is clearly taught in Philippians 4:6-7, *"Be careful for nothing; but in everything by prayer and supplication with thanks-*

giving let your requests be made known unto God. And the peace of God, which passeth all understanding, shall keep your hearts and minds through Christ Jesus."

Verses three and four in II Peter describe why this faith is called a precious faith. When a person accepts Jesus Christ as their Savior they have all they need. *". . .You are complete in Him. . ."* (Colossians 2:10). This is so remarkable. When I have Jesus I have everything. When you have Jesus you have everything! This takes place by the divine power of God. Based on this gift God then provides precious promises. These promises are of great value. The apostle's life that was described in the beginning of this book helped him to grasp the preciousness of his faith. He writes about precious faith in his epistle. *"That the trial of your faith, being much more precious than of gold that perisheth, though it be tried with fire, might be found unto praise and honor and glory at the appearing of Jesus Christ"* (I Peter 1:7). In II Peter 1:1, he speaks of precious promises, *"Simon Peter, a servant and an apostle of Jesus Christ, to them that have obtained like precious faith with us through the righteousness of God and our Savior Jesus Christ"*. Additionally he mentions *"the precious blood"* (I Peter 1:19). "The precious stone" is stated (I Peter 2:4,6) and above all there is *"the precious Savior"* (I Peter 2:7).

Verse four describes to us the divine nature. The world experiences corruption. Lost people have different interests that lead to emptiness. God's people experience a new nature that is God's nature. Since this is the nature of God it gives direction to our lifestyle. This nature needs to be fed. The feeding is from the Word of God. A godly life and lifestyle is from the feeding that takes place. It is revealed in the outgrowth of how a believer lives.

When a person accepts Christ as their Savior we sometimes call it the new birth. A birth is the commencement, the beginning of life. The apostle now lists seven attributes (characteristics) of godly living. The key word in verse five is "add." The term is not speaking of mathematical adding but it refers to the supply that is available from God. He is speaking here of growth. The question is, 'how are you growing?'

Notice the attributes. The first is excellence (virtue). In Greek philosophy virtue had the concept of a "fulfillment". When something fulfills its purpose it has moral excellence. When we look at a job in process or finished we might say, "That is excellent." This is not speaking about fixing up our human abilities but it refers to the nature of divinity living through our lives. It is not us. It is the Living Christ through us.

The next word is knowledge. The knowledge in verses two and three refers to a fulfillment of knowledge. The word here suggests practical knowledge. How well are you handling life? It is the Word of God affecting our thinking and our lives become changed.

The next term is temperance. The term means "self control." It speaks to discipline. Just as the musician must practice, the athlete must train so the child of God must develop discipline.

Patience is so important. This is one of my great struggles. Tough times come to all of us. Patience is the God given ability to endure through tough times. Trials are a part of life. They happen personally, in ministry, and at the work place. Trials build patience. No one likes trials. They do come.

Godliness is an interesting term. It carries with it the idea of worshipping well! A person like this will live above the petty, mundane minutia of life. This person seeks to live unto God and seek the welfare of others. These individuals are often sought out. This person attempts to do what is right, not just what is convenient.

From godliness comes brotherly kindness. Loving others is a challenge. This is a great evidence of the born again experience. This leads to love. The word for love here is *agape* love. In the apostle's day there were two primary words used for love. The first was *eros*. This spoke of passionate love. This was a sexual love of the flesh. The other was *phileo*. This describes love between friends. When Paul penned the great love chapter of I Corinthians 13 a new word was selected. This word was new. This love is one that reaches out to everyone. It is a command to love God and one another. The model of this is Jesus (John 15:12). Love is the ingredient that is indispensible to properly use the spiritual gifts given to individuals. Without love that which we do is of little value. We can only learn this love from God (I John 4:19).

These characteristics are the product of God working in a believer's life. The divine nature works within our lives.

The Christian Life is a Fruitful Life – II Peter 1:8-11

The apostle now lists characteristics of how the Christian life works. The first is fruitfulness abounding. The word barren means ineffective. Now this fruitfulness is not something we muster up. It is cultivated and produced as we yield to Christ through obedience to His word.

When we do not grow we become short sighted (1:9). Our fruitfulness should not only abound but it should grow as we visualize how big God's kingdom work is. The church of Jesus Christ must mentor the next generation. We must see beyond our family, church, denomination, our group! When we look at Christianity as our little group we are not seeing the big picture and our mentality will become very 'cultic!' We need to open our eyes and see the big picture!

Now verses ten and eleven bring us to the theme of this section. Our calling and election needs to be sure. As we grow our salvation becomes deeper and spiritual immaturity will slowly give way to Biblical maturity. The Christian life is the work of God in our lives.

Verse 11 is a reference to the Greek athletic games. The abundant entrance into God's eternal kingdom will be a deep seeded confidence for God's people. The word 'supplied' here from the New King James Version comes from a musical term. When the groups sang there would be an underwriter. Someone would put up provision for the concert. God has given us provision through Jesus Christ.

There are so many blessings for the child of God. Beyond the earthly blessing is heaven. Now too shabby! So make sure of your calling and election!

Questions:

1. The key word to understanding the Christian life is

   _____.

2. The Greek word *kai* means? It can also be rendered as

   _____.

3. What are the elements Peter says are precious?

Discussion:

1. What are the signs of fruitfulness that found in your life?

Chapter 12

THINGS THAT ARE IMPORTANT
II Peter 1:12-21

"For this reason I will not be negligent to remind you always of these things, though you know and are established in the present truth. Yes, I think it is right, as long as I am in this tent, to stir you up by reminding you, knowing that shortly I must put off my tent, just as our Lord Jesus Christ showed me. Moreover I will be careful to ensure that you always have a reminder of these things after my decease. For we did not follow cunningly devised fables when we made known to you the power and coming of our Lord Jesus Christ, but were eyewitnesses of His majesty. For He received from God the Father honor and glory when such a voice came to Him from the Excellent Glory: "This is My beloved Son, in whom I am well pleased." And we heard this voice which came from heaven when we were with Him on the holy mountain. And so we have the prophetic word confirmed, which you do well to heed as a light that shines in a dark place, until the day dawns and the morning star rises in your hearts; knowing this first, that no prophecy of Scripture is of any private interpretation, for prophecy never came by the will of man, but holy men of God spoke as they were moved by the Holy Spirit." **(II Peter 1:12-21)**

I was chatting with my wife recently and we were on a particular subject. I went completely off course in the conversation and talked on another topic. "Why did you say that?" my wife asked with a surprised look on her face and I responded that it was passing through my mind and I needed to say it then or I would forget it! We both laughed. Remembering is a very important issue.

Peter in the early part of this chapter presented Christian lifestyle and now he proceeds to discuss our authority which is God's Word.

The Importance of Remembering – II Peter 1:12-15

In verses 12-15 he uses the word 'remembrance' three times. He lists three things to remember

The first is found in the word negligent. Peter was obedient to Christ's command and he encourages the readers to be obedient. Peter had a ministry to fulfill. *"Most assuredly, I say to you, when you were younger, you girded yourself and walked where you wished; but when you are old, you will stretch out your hands, and another will gird you and carry you where you do not wish"* (John 21:18). Jesus was explaining to Peter how he would die. Tradition tells us that Peter died the death of crucifixion and that he died upside down on a cross. He knew that Christ gave him another chance to serve Him and he was determined to be faithful to his calling. He did not want to be negligent.

The second thing to remember is that we are here for a brief period of time. He uses the metaphor of his body like a tabernacle. Here, but gone soon! Verse fourteen is a reminder of what Jesus told Peter in the record of John 21:18.

The third thing to remember is in verse 15. The word *"endeavor"* (KJV) is the same word translated in some passages as diligence (II Peter 1:5, 10). It means to "do something quickly." Peter knew he would die soon and he had spiritual responsibilities to take care of. A good exercise is to list things that you would like to do before you die. There are a number of things I personally have written in my mind that I would like to do before I die. For example there are a number of things I would like to write. I am motivated to rise early in the morning to go to the basement of our house to write books and articles. I must do this! That is my heart.

In verse 13 Peter uses the term "stir up." The term means to "to wake up with a reminder." It means "get with it"! It is easy to take things for granted. We must remember. The Holy Spirit's work helps us to remember.

Peter had the greatest of blessings. He would leave behind the inspired Word of God. He wrote I and II Peter and they are divinely inspired – God breathed truth from God.

The Importance of Experiences – II Peter 1:16-18

Peter remembered some amazing experiences he had with Christ. One such experience was the transfiguration. It is interesting to note that the three synoptic gospels record the event. Matthew, Mark, and Luke, however, were not there when it happened. Peter was!

Peter uses the word *"tabernacle"* in verses 13 and 14 to speak of his own flesh. He writes of his *"decease"* in verse 15. The word means "exodus." Moses led the nation of Israel out from Egypt toward the Promised Land and it is commonly called the exodus. You will notice he uses the personal pronoun "I" in verses 12-15. In verse 16 he uses the word "we." You will recall that at the transfiguration appeared Moses, Elijah along with Jesus and Peter, James, and John. Death is an exodus from this life to another. Peter recalls this by remembering the great men of God, Moses and Elijah, who had deceased (exodus) many years prior.

There are several significant issues here.

Moses and Elijah represent the Law and the Prophets. The Father's message from heaven, *"This is my beloved Son in whom I am well pleased,"* emphasized that Christ Jesus death would lead to glory. Another issue is that this would fulfill Jesus promise that some would see the kingdom prior to death (Matthew 16:28; Mark 9:1; Luke 9:27). The three, Peter, James, and John now saw what the kingdom was like.

Peter takes these significant issues and begins to describe the challenges of false religion that was abounding in the days of Peter. The fables listed in verse 16 are myths. The transfiguration was no myth! Peter tells his story. Jesus in majestic, regal glory was seen! He heard the words of the Father. God the Father told Peter, James, and John that Jesus, the carpenter's son, born of the youthful Mary is in fact the Son of God.

Jesus Christ accomplished the victory in this decease. He accomplished the salvation of lost sinners. Our salvation promises us that when we exodus we go on into glory with our Lord.

Each of us has experiences. I am sure none of us have had the experience of Peter in the transfiguration. But we do have ours!

The Importance of God's Word – II Peter 1:19-21

Remembering is important. Experience is a teacher. Peter is declaring, however, the Scripture is better than the experience he enjoyed with James and John on the Mount of Transfiguration. The Scriptures in their entirety, all 66 books written over 1500 years by nearly 40 authors are our final authority. There are numerous promises of the authority of Scripture.

"How can a young man cleanse his way? By taking heed according to Your word. With my whole heart I have sought You; oh, let me not wander from Your commandments! Your word I have hidden in my heart, that I might not sin against You" (Psalm 119:9-11).

"Blessed is the man who walks not in the counsel of the ungodly, nor stands in the path of sinners, nor sits in the seat of the scornful; but his delight is in the law of the Lord, and in His law he meditates day and night. He shall be like a tree planted by the rivers of water, that brings forth its fruit in its season, whose leaf also shall not wither; and whatever he does shall prosper" (Psalm 1:1-3).

"The law of the Lord is perfect, converting the soul; the testimony of the Lord is sure, making wise the simple" (Psalm 19:7).

"Therefore all Your precepts concerning all things I consider to be right; I hate every false way" (Psalm 119:128).

The Word is spoken of as a "light that shineth in a dark place." *"That was the true Light which gives light to every man coming into the world. He was in the world, and the world was made through Him, and the world did not know Him. He came to His own, and His own did not receive Him"* (John 1:9-11); *"Your word is a lamp to my feet and a light to my path"* (Psalm 119:105); *"The people who sat in darkness have seen a great light, and upon those who sat in the region and shadow of death light has dawned"* (Matthew 4:16).

The world gets darker but we must be the light. The phrase "until the day dawns" is a reference to the sun that comes up in the east after a dark night as a metaphor of the Word of God shining brightly in our lives.

The Bible is divinely inspired. I oversee a wonderful college that is a school of biblical higher education. Davis College has held to a Biblical worldview for over 100 years. Divine inspiration is at the heart of our college. It is the foundation of Davis College. The word inspired means "God breathed." Although God used the writers of Scriptures with their unique personalities the Bible is a book directly from God. Verse 21 tells us that the writers were moved by the Holy Spirit. The concept is that they were carried along. Like a father carries a child or a wind carries a ship, God's writers were led by the Holy Spirit.

One of the issues of II Peter is that the apostle was addressing apostates. Chapter 2 teaches that they twisted the Scripture and a prime characteristic of this was denying prophecy. Look at II Peter 3:3-4, *"knowing this first: that scoffers will come in the last days, walking according to their own lusts, and saying, "Where is the promise of His coming? For since the fathers fell asleep, all things continue as they were from the beginning of creation."*

A key to understanding Peter's emphasis is found in the term private interpretation. The word means "unto self." The Scripture is to be connected and is linked together. Scripture should not be used to isolate a certain verse and come to a conclusion that is neither connected nor biblical. The Bible is one book, connected together, telling the story of God.

Experiences fade and often become embellished. The Word of God lasts. The children in Bible Studies sing that little song "The B-I-B-L-E, yes that's the book for me. I stand alone on the Word of God – The B-I-B-L-E!" This is what we need to remember.

One of my greatest joys in life is to see someone come to Jesus Christ in salvation. I love to see it. Often there is no interest and then as the Bible, God's Word is presented, I see it. Often there is a tear, a lump in their throat and shortly they are praying to receive Christ.

It is an amazing experience. Often I read the Word and something seems to leap off the page to me. It is God using His Word by the Holy Spirit.

Peter wants to make it clear. The Bible is the Word of God. Now he is about to warn us about the counterfeits!

Questions:
1. What experience did Peter reflect on in this chapter?
2. Who appeared at the transfiguration?
3. What is divine inspiration of scripture?

Discussion:
1. What experiences have been the highlights in your Christian journey?

Chapter 13

WATCH OUT FOR FRAUDS
II Peter 2:1-22

"But there were also false prophets among the people, even as there will be false teachers among you, who will secretly bring in destructive heresies, even denying the Lord who bought them, and bring on themselves swift destruction. And many will follow their destructive ways, because of whom the way of truth will be blasphemed. By covetousness they will exploit you with deceptive words; for a long time their judgment has not been idle, and their destruction does not slumber. For if God did not spare the angels who sinned, but cast them down to hell and delivered them into chains of darkness, to be reserved for judgment; and did not spare the ancient world, but saved Noah, one of eight people, a preacher of righteousness, bringing in the flood on the world of the ungodly; and turning the cities of Sodom and Gomorrah into ashes, condemned them to destruction, making them an example to those who afterward would live ungodly; and delivered righteous Lot, who was oppressed by the filthy conduct of the wicked (for that righteous man, dwelling among them, tormented his righteous soul from day to day by seeing and hearing their lawless deeds)— then the Lord knows how to deliver the godly out of temptations and to reserve the unjust under punishment for the day of judgment. Who once were not a people but are now the people of God, who had not obtained mercy but now have obtained mercy. Beloved, I beg you as sojourners and pil-

grims, abstain from fleshly lusts which war against the soul, having your conduct honorable among the Gentiles, that when they speak against you as evildoers, they may, by your good works which they observe, glorify God in the day of visitation. Therefore submit your-selves to every ordinance of man for the Lord's sake, whether to the king as supreme, or to governors, as to those who are sent by him for the punishment of evildoers and for the praise of those who do good. For this is the will of God, that by doing good you may put to silence the ignorance of foolish men— as free, yet not using liberty as a cloak for vice, but as bondservants of God. Honor all people. Love the brotherhood. Fear God. Honor the king. Servants, be submissive to your masters with all fear, not only to the good and gentle, but also to the harsh. For this is commendable, if because of conscience toward God one endures grief, suffering wrongfully. For what credit is it if, when you are beaten for your faults, you take it patiently? But when you do good and suffer, if you take it patiently, this is com-mendable before God. For to this you were called, because Christ also suffered for us, leaving us an example, that you should follow His steps: "Who committed no sin, Nor was deceit found in His mouth" **(II Peter 2:1-9)**

*C*ounterfeiting began when Satan started the concept by deceiving Eve in the Garden of Eden (Genesis 3). I do not remember where I heard it but someone told me that investigators who find counterfeiters do so by studying the real thing. In other words, an investigator can spot the fraud because he is so familiar with the real thing.

The Scriptures often remind us of counterfeiting. Satan con-tinues to offer the counterfeit. *"Oh, that you would bear with me in a little folly—and indeed you do bear with me. For I am jealous for you with godly jealousy. For I have betrothed you to one hus-band, that I may present you as a chaste virgin to Christ. But I fear, lest somehow, as the serpent deceived Eve by his craftiness, so your minds may be corrupted from the simplicity that is in Christ. For if he who comes preaches another Jesus whom we have not preached, or if you receive a different spirit which you have not received, or a different gospel which you have not accepted—you may well put up with it!"* (II Corinthians 11:1-4); *"I marvel that you are turning away so soon from Him who called you in the grace of Christ, to a different gospel, which is not another; but there are some who trouble you and want to pervert the gospel of Christ. But even if we, or an angel from heaven, preach any other gospel to you than what we have preached to you, let him be accursed. As we have said before, so now I say again, if anyone preaches any other gospel to you than what you have received, let him be accursed"* (Galatians 1:6-9). One day the false Christ will appear as it says in II Thessalonians 2:3-4, *"let no one deceive you by any means; for that Day will not come unless the falling away comes first, and the man of sin is revealed, the son of perdition, who opposes and exalts himself above all that is called God or that is worshiped, so that he sits as God in the temple of God, showing himself that he is God."*

Peter was very familiar with false teachers. False teachers have a motive that has nothing to do with bringing glory to God.

Sighting a False Teacher – II Peter 2:1-3

Peter is very clear. There will be people who teach "damnable heresies." The term means they will teach things that are destructive to the well being of the learners. The word heresy has a broad meaning. It refers to a teaching that is contrary to the 'precious faith' Peter wrote about in chapter 1 and it separates one from the precious promises he spoke of in 1:4. Sects, Cults, and false religions are the result of this type of teaching. The word heresy actually refers to decisions and choices. When a church separates itself from Biblical doctrine or challenges leadership about the church's direction (unless it is unbiblical) it produces divisiveness in the body of Christ.

Often when someone is involved in teaching something that is false the approach is to make it look similar. Shortly the basis of truth is dismissed. When examining false teachers the method seems plausible but when the error is discovered usually the motive and the method was wrong as well.

It is interesting to note that they bring in the teaching secretly. Ultimately the teaching is revealed as false. The basis of purity in a body of believers is the doctrine that is proclaimed. What is being taught needs to line up with the Biblical position and most Christian ministries are able to outline the doctrinal position.

In verse one Peter describes these false teachers by what they do not believe. Commonly held Biblical doctrines are denied. It is always interesting to note that the crux of their denial usually surrounds the deity of Jesus Christ. The heart of the Christian faith is the gospel. Look at I Corinthians 15:1-4, *"moreover, brethren, I declare to you the gospel which I preached to you, which also you received and in which you stand, by which also you are saved, if you hold fast that word which I preached to you—unless you believed in vain. For I delivered to you first of all that which I also received: that Christ died for our sins according to the Scriptures, and that He was buried, and that He rose again the third day according to the Scriptures."* Apologist William Lane Craig states that this was the "creed of the early church." The term "bought" then does not seem to mean that they were saved. It does refer to the fact that Jesus died for the sins of the world and potentially all can be saved. Salvation is limited to those who believe. The word atonement refers to the covering of all our sins. It is efficient only to those who believe. All Christians, all true followers of Christ agree that Jesus Christ is the God man who only can forgive sins based on His atoning work on the cross. As English cleric Herbert Lockyer put it, "The Son of God became the Son of man that sons of men might become the sons of God."

A description of these false teachers is found in the word *pernicious* (vv. 2). The word refers to their conduct. These are individuals who use the guise of religion for what they consider some sort of gain. They could be in a small church promoting havoc or they could be in front of huge crowds. I always liked to have big crowds. The more the better possibility someone would be saved. However, big never means better nor does it even mean right! It is because of these types of individuals mentioned by Peter that the work of God gets such shame. The world, the media of the world and numerous friends of the world hold these individuals and their teaching up to give evidence that the message of Christ is incorrect.

The ultimate motive for a false teacher is money. They exploit, exploit, and exploit! Giving to God's work is essential. My wife and I have practiced tithing and the giving of offerings for years. These gifts, however, are not for my gain! The teaching that God wants everyone rich is inconceivable and not practical. Jesus gave up all the riches of heaven to be a poor man on earth. The apostles were not in it for gain but to serve. It was Peter who went with John up to the gate called Beautiful and they met a lame man asking for money. It was Peter who said *"Silver and gold I do not have, but what I do have I give you: In the name of Jesus Christ of Nazareth, rise up and walk"* (Acts 3:6). Peter was not cleverly trying to get any gain. In fact he admitted he had no money to give. The prophet Micah's searching words *"Her heads judge for a bribe. . ."* (Micah 3:11). God's preachers and workers are to be properly compensated. If someone is in God's work for money it is very dangerous.

Another part of false teaching is the kind of words that are used. "Feigned" words carry the idea of plastic. Plastic breaks easily. This type of preaching is for the ego of the hearers. When religion is erroneously used it can be exploitation for the weak.

Preachers and Christian leaders need to live their lives in such a way that their message is consistent with their words. Humanly, that is impossible. We need the leading and directing of the Holy Spirit working through the life of God's preachers and leaders.

The End of the False Prophet – II Peter 2:4-11

Entitlements and tolerance are very common words that have been sighted in the Postmodern Era. Entitlement carries with it the idea of "you owe me". Tolerance depicts "you believe what you want and I will believe what I want and we'll all be OK!" Both teachings are anti biblical.

The epistle of II Peter indicates that these concepts are drawn from false prophets and their doom is sealed. He uses two illustrations. The first is the fallen angels. Look at Isaiah 14:12-15, *"How you are fallen from heaven, O Lucifer, son of the morning! How you are cut down to the ground, you who weakened the nations! For you have said in your heart: 'I will ascend into heaven, I will exalt my throne above the stars of God; I will also sit on the mount of the con-*

gregation on the farthest sides of the north; I will ascend above the heights of the clouds, I will be like the Most High.' Yet you shall be brought down to Sheol, to the lowest depths of the Pit." This passage describes the fall of Lucifer. Lucifer was evidently next to God and perhaps was in charge of the angelic hosts. Pride gripped his spirit and he wished to have what did not belong to him. A sad situation is to see a subordinate attempt to take something from his superior. Satan began this disloyalty. Satan led the charge against God. Following him were the fallen angels. The Bible indicates the angels are the demons of this world. "Be sober, be vigilant; because your adversary the devil walks about like a roaring lion, seeking whom he may devour" (I Peter 5:8); *"Finally, my brethren, be strong in the Lord and in the power of His might. Put on the whole armor of God, that you may be able to stand against the wiles of the devil. For we do not wrestle against flesh and blood, but against principalities, against powers, against the rulers of the darkness of this age, against spiritual hosts of wickedness in the heavenly places"* (Ephesians 6:10-12). There are also other fallen angels who are subscribed by God to Tartarus. The word means the underworld. Perhaps this is a special section of eternity in hell and these angels are chained and they are waiting for the final judgment. So the parallel is if God has judged rebellious angels He will do so with rebellious teachers.

Secondly, there is the illustration and parallel of the Noahic flood. In this amazing biblical episode Noah and his family, just eight people, are able to survive the first flood of human history. The world was wicked and God's edict was to start fresh! One of the characteristics of Noah's day was business as usual. Luke 17:26-27 says, *"and as it was in the days of Noah, so it will be also in the days of the Son of Man: they ate, they drank, they married wives, they were given in marriage, until the day that Noah entered the ark, and the flood came and destroyed them all."* The people did 'their thing.' As it says in Genesis 6:3, the population was exploding. *"And the Lord said, "My Spirit shall not strive with man forever, for he is indeed flesh; yet his days shall be one hundred and twenty years".* Wickedness and complacency reigned, *"then the Lord saw that the wickedness of man was great in the earth, and that every intent of the thoughts of his heart was only evil continually"* (Genesis 6:5).

Violence was part of the norm of the age, *"The earth also was corrupt before God, and the earth was filled with violence . . . And God said to Noah, "The end of all flesh has come before Me, for the earth is filled with violence through them; and behold, I will destroy them with the earth"* (Genesis 6:11,13). Followers of Elohim were the minority. The flood came. God's judgment was on all those who refused to obey the truth.

Another tragedy that doomed the fate of God rejecters was Sodom and Gomorrah (2:6-9). Peter describes the people of that day as lawless (2:8). Moses gave the law later so this lawlessness was against the very nature that God had given. Here was sexual behavior that was perverted. Sodomy is unnatural. Abraham prayed and begged with God that if there could be some righteous found he would request the Almighty to spare the people. There simply were not ten righteous to be found. God sent brimstone and fire. Genesis 19:24 says, *"Then the Lord rained brimstone and fire on Sodom and Gomorrah, from the Lord out of the heavens."* On the road to Petra there is a spot where pilgrims of that area believe it is possible that the judgment of God came. Some Biblical teachers believe the judgment came on the city and it is buried under the Dead Sea.

Three illustrations of judgment are listed. They are the fallen angels, the flood, and Sodom and Gomorrah. They remind us of the fact that God judges. Beware of those who do not teach the truth and pervert the teachings that surround our blessed Lord and Savior, Jesus Christ.

The Deliverance of True Believers – II Peter 2:5-9

This section of Scripture also contrasts that the people of God want to be delivered. Noah is cited as a man who for 120 years proclaimed the truth of what was known of God up to that time. He was in the world but a light for God to the world. We live in a sin polluted world. Sin abounds everywhere. This was a tough world to raise a family in! Somehow three wives were found for Noah's sons. When judgment came there was an ark of safety. When we have Jesus Christ as our Savior, He is our safety. God's promise is that the world will never be destroyed again by a flood. The beauty of a rainbow following a rain fall is the reminder to the world of safe keeping.

Lot was a righteous man. When his uncle Abram left the Ur of the Chaldees, he took with him Lot. Unfortunately, Lot fell into the world and became more and more like them. Look at Genesis 13:12, *"Abram dwelt in the land of Canaan, and Lot dwelt in the cities of the plain and pitched his tent even as far as Sodom"*. He eventually moved into the city of Sodom as it says in Genesis 14:12, *"They also took Lot, Abram's brother's son who dwelt in Sodom, and his goods, and departed"*. Evidently that is where his heart was. We must be careful to learn that while we are in the world, we should not be like the world! His daughters were influenced and married into the families of Sodom. When it came time to leave Sodom, his son-in-laws ridiculed the warning that was given. The issue here is that even when we are in tough situations we can live godly in Christ Jesus. Perhaps your husband is unsaved or you work where you are persecuted, or you have a child that has separated themselves from Christ or another type of issue has come into your life, remember that Jesus loves you unconditionally and He wants you to stay close to Him.

It seems to me that we see God's gracious favor by His desire to rescue Lot from the difficult situation. Here in Sodom people were 'living it up' and when judgment came they were not prepared for what was coming!

When Christians and churches compromise with the world the message of truth is weakened. God will deliver, but we must be strong in the grace of God. Dietrich Bonhoeffer, the German pastor, spy, prophet, and martyr once said, "Silence in the face of evil is itself evil: God will not hold us guiltless. Not to speak is to speak. Not to act is to act."

The Results of False Teaching – II Peter 2:10-16
Peter began his second epistle with encouraging words to believers. In this section the apostle describes false teachers. He does not name them specifically. He describes their errors and the results of their teaching.

Their Actions – II Peter 2:10-12

The description of these individuals is very unique. They always try to build themselves up while tearing others down. 'Make others look bad' is their motto. We all are depraved and need to have the righteousness of Christ applied to our lives. The motto 'watch out for number one' means take care of yourself. Apostasy has a tendency to always think of self first. Peter then describes these people as presumptuous. This speaks of their 'boldness' to promote number one. Self willed means 'to please self! Inwardly they fed their egos. They live to attack leaders. The word for dignitaries in verse ten is a reference to spiritual leaders. The context seems to even refer to the angels in verse 11. There is a major spiritual war always taking place. I have observed in my ministry that where God is doing a great work and abundance is about to come then look out, the devil and his cohorts are about to attack! It is interesting to note that the context of this passage seems to refer to the fact that godly angels do not bring accusation against fallen angels. It appears to me that we are better off to promote the light of truth instead of always cursing the darkness! Speaking evil of others, telling stories to make someone look bad, or pointing the finger is to be avoided. In the political arena of America there needs to be an explanation of views and issues but it becomes somewhat embarrassing when leaders always attack the person.

"Remind them to be subject to rulers and authorities, to obey, to be ready for every good work, to speak evil of no one, to be peaceable, gentle, showing all humility to all men" (Titus 3:1-2);

"Let every soul be subject to the governing authorities. For there is no authority except from God, and the authorities that exist are appointed by God. Therefore whoever resists the authority resists the ordinance of God, and those who resist will bring judgment on themselves. For rulers are not a terror to good works, but to evil. Do you want to be unafraid of the authority? Do what is good, and you will have praise from the same. For he is God's minister to you for good. But if you do evil, be afraid; for he does not bear the sword in

vain; for he is God's minister, an avenger to execute wrath on him who practices evil. Therefore you must be subject, not only because of wrath but also for conscience' sake. For because of this you also pay taxes, for they are God's ministers attending continually to this very thing. Render therefore to all their due: taxes to whom taxes are due, customs to whom customs, fear to whom fear, honor to whom honor. Owe no one anything except to love one another, for he who loves another has fulfilled the law. For the commandments, "You shall not commit adultery," "You shall not murder," "You shall not steal," "You shall not bear false witness," "You shall not covet," and if there is any other commandment, are all summed up in this saying, namely, "You shall love your neighbor as yourself." Love does no harm to a neighbor; therefore love is the fulfillment of the law. And do this, knowing the time, that now it is high time to awake out of sleep; for now our salvation is nearer than when we first believed. The night is far spent, the day is at hand. Therefore let us cast off the works of darkness, and let us put on the armor of light. Let us walk properly, as in the day, not in revelry and drunkenness, not in lewdness and lust, not in strife and envy. But put on the Lord Jesus Christ, and make no provision for the flesh, to fulfill its lusts" (Romans 13).

The example of the apostles was not one of attacking the leaders but of dealing with the truth about issues.

God describes these as "brute beasts" and their destination is destruction. Look at the following verses in II Peter 2, *"then the Lord knows how to deliver the godly out of temptations and to reserve the unjust under punishment for the day of judgment"* (2:9); *"But these, like natural brute beasts made to be caught and destroyed, speak evil of the things they do not understand, and will utterly perish in their own corruption"* (2:12); *"These are wells without water, clouds carried by a tempest, for whom is reserved the blackness of darkness forever"* (2:17); *"and especially those who walk according to the flesh in the lust of uncleanness and despise authority. They are presumptuous, self-willed. They are not afraid to speak evil of dignitaries"* (2:20). Destruction is an awful end. They speak evil of things outside of their scope of understanding. Often these individuals enjoy luxurious living, *"by covetousness they will exploit you with deceptive words; for a long time their judgment has not been idle, and their destruction does not slumber"* (II Peter 2:3). Often a teaching emerges that promises great wealth if one aims for it. When one always talks about "I, me, and my" and promotes a class above others it is an example of motives that are not righteous.

These are described as carousers. A false belief system leads to a false Biblical worldview. A false worldview leads to a faulty life-style. These teachers always talk about "so what is wrong with—". These teachers make it easier for people to sin. Christian love and grace are not vehicles to promote sin.

Verse fourteen is very potent, *"having eyes full of adultery and that cannot cease from sin, enticing unstable souls. They have a heart trained in covetous practices, and are accursed children"*. These false teachers are in the midst for two reasons. First, they attempt to satisfy their own nature and to fulfill their own lusts and secondly, their goal to capture 'unstable' souls. *"For of this sort are those who creep into households and make captives of gullible women loaded down with sins, led away by various lusts"* (II Timothy 3:6). Pastors need to be very careful in counseling sessions with the opposite sex. Often adultery results and great harm and lust are developed.

The term "enticing unstable souls" in verse 14 would be very familiar to Peter. It is a fisherman's term depicting the idea of placing the bait on a hook. It also is a hunter's image of baiting a trap. Now in the context of this passage of Scripture Peter is addressing how apostates and false teachers manipulate and deceive people. They use one of the most precious doctrines in Scripture and pervert it. It is the doctrine of the grace of God. At the beginning of the II epistle to Peter, the apostle addresses "like precious faith" (1:1). He then proclaims the common introductory remark of 'grace' (1:2). He teaches us that grace and peace be 'multiplied' in the 'knowledge of God and of Jesus our Lord' (1:2). History teaches that there are many who take grace and pervert it with the teaching that the more one sins there is always ample grace to sin. It is called antinomianism. Antinomy is the contradiction between two valid principles.

It becomes an irresolvable conflict. One who holds this position identifies that under the gospel dispensation the practicing out of the truth has no place. It is true that grace through faith is alone necessary to our salvation. But we must take all of the scripture to heart. Look at Ephesians 2:8-10, *"for by grace you have been saved through faith, and that not of yourselves; it is the gift of God, not of works, lest anyone should boast. For we are His workmanship, created in Christ Jesus for good works, which God prepared beforehand that we should walk in them."* Our salvation is based on Christ completely. Once we have come to Christ our love for Him changes how we live. This type of liberty that was evident in Peter's day becomes self centered and self serving. Our goal is not to be free but to serve our Master, Jesus Christ. The freedom we have is freedom from sin to serve our dear Lord. Just as an athlete strives to discipline himself so a believer desires to live out his faith. Many precious people are raised in legalistic families. In church they were taught to live a certain way and somehow by doing this thought God would love them more. God, the Father, loves us because of Jesus Christ, God the Son, who paid for our sins. Sometimes there are individuals who come from abused families and reject things of God because they have been so hurt. These dear ones can find what they need in Christ.

Peter speaks about those who proclaim 'freedom with no responsibility' as 'unstable souls.' This is a key reason for Christians to be in good, solid Bible centered churches and in groups that can help them grow in the Lord. He readers of this epistle in Peter's day were established in the faith (II Peter 1:12). Nevertheless he warned them of this dangerous and false teaching.

In II Peter 2, Peter clearly points out that these false teachers have a desire to receive personal gain *"by covetousness they will exploit you with deceptive words; for a long time their judgment has not been idle, and their destruction does not slumber"* (2:3), *"having eyes full of adultery and that cannot cease from sin, enticing unstable souls. They have a heart trained in covetous practices, and are accursed children"* (2:14). They become masters at deceit!

As I write this commentary and have preached through I and II Peter in Bible conferences several times it has reminded me of the many, many servants of God I know. Not one of them has ever given the concept that they are after money! In this passage, Peter explains that the bottom line desire of these false prophets is covetousness. To covet is to desire jealously what belongs to another. It is an inordinate and unhealthy desire for wealth! It is not wrong to have money or wealth. I Timothy 6:17-19 says, *"Command those who are rich in this present age not to be haughty, nor to trust in uncertain riches but in the living God, who gives us richly all things to enjoy. Let them do good, that they be rich in good works, ready to give, willing to share, storing up for themselves a good foundation for the time to come, that they may lay hold on eternal life"*. It is no wonder that people who teach freedom do so with such conviction for it enables them to strive to fulfill their desire to be popular and to enhance their own revenue.

It is interesting to note that Peter uses the illustration of Balaam in verse 15 and 16. The king of Moab, Balak, feared the Jewish people. He turned to Balaam to help him. Balaam was covetous and this Gentile prophet followed the way of evil and began to curse the Jews. God told Balaam not to help Balak. Balaam kept prompting God and God tested Balaam by allowing him to go to the princess. Balaam began to go astray. God did one of the unique things found in the Scriptures. God had his donkey rebuke him. Eventually, God allowed Balaam to set up altars. Look at Dueteronomy 23:4-5, *"because they did not meet you with bread and water on the road when you came out of Egypt, and because they hired against you Balaam the son of Beor from Pethor of Mesopotamia, to curse you. Nevertheless the Lord your God would not listen to Balaam, but the Lord your God turned the curse into a blessing for you, because the Lord your God loves you"*. Balaam tells Balak how to defeat the nation of Israel. Balaam, like these false prophets in Peter's day lusted to be known and desired to have what was not his (covetousness), when he confessed his sin (Numbers 22:34) it was evidently not sincere. Because of his following and leading Israel to such heartache, Balaam was slain by a sword. He rebelled against God.

Peter addresses this as 'madness.' Balaam was deranged.

A servant of God desires to serve others. We all must be wary of such infiltrators into God's Kingdom work. Christian leaders need to be watchful and careful to not fall into this trap.

Watch Out For Freedom – II Peter 2:17-22

Freedom costs! Those who worked at freeing the slaves in British and American history went through major problems. Freedom costs. Ask Abraham Lincoln or Martin Luther King who sacrificed their lives. Most important, see it in the life of our blessed Savior.

Apostates offer a freedom that actually leads to bondage.

The False Promise – II Peter 2:17-18

To have faith is one thing. Where that faith is directed is critical! Faith must be in someone reliable. Peter lists three metaphors to emphasize the empty promises and results from false teachers. He calls them "wells without water." A spring without water, a creek dried up is of no value. People need God. Jesus described this need beautifully when He met the Samaritan woman. Read slowly the passage and sense what the Lord is offering to her.

"But He needed to go through Samaria. So He came to a city of Samaria which is called Sychar, near the plot of ground that Jacob gave to his son Joseph. 6 Now Jacob's well was there. Jesus therefore, being wearied from His journey, sat thus by the well. It was about the sixth hour. A woman of Samaria came to draw water. Jesus said to her, "Give Me a drink." For His disciples had gone away into the city to buy food. Then the woman of Samaria said to Him, "How is it that You, being a Jew, ask a drink from me, a Samaritan woman?" For Jews have no dealings with Samaritans. Jesus answered and said to her, "If you knew the gift of God, and who it is who says to you, 'Give Me a drink,' you would have asked Him, and He would have given you living water." The woman said to Him, "Sir, You have nothing to draw with, and the well is deep. Where then do You get that living water? Are You greater than our father Jacob, who gave us the well, and drank from it himself, as well as his sons and

his livestock?" Jesus answered and said to her, "Whoever drinks of this water will thirst again, 14 but whoever drinks of the water that I shall give him will never thirst. But the water that I shall give him will become in him a fountain of water springing up into everlasting life." The woman said to Him, "Sir, give me this water, that I may not thirst, nor come here to draw." Jesus said to her, "Go, call your husband, and come here." The woman answered and said, "I have no husband." Jesus said to her, "You have well said, 'I have no husband,' for you have had five husbands, and the one whom you now have is not your husband; in that you spoke truly." The woman said to Him, "Sir, I perceive that You are a prophet. 20 Our fathers worshiped on this mountain, and you Jews say that in Jerusalem is the place where one ought to worship." Jesus said to her, "Woman, believe Me, the hour is coming when you will neither on this mountain, nor in Jerusalem, worship the Father. You worship what you do not know; we know what we worship, for salvation is of the Jews. But the hour is coming, and now is, when the true worshipers will worship the Father in spirit and truth; for the Father is seeking such to worship Him. God is Spirit, and those who worship Him must worship in spirit and truth." The woman said to Him, "I know that Messiah is coming" (who is called Christ). "When He comes, He will tell us all things." Jesus said to her, "I who speak to you am He." And at this point His disciples came, and they marveled that He talked with a woman; yet no one said, "What do You seek?" or, "Why are You talking with her?" The woman then left her waterpot, went her way into the city, and said to the men, "Come, see a Man who told me all things that I ever did. Could this be the Christ?" (John 4:4-29)

You can find in Jesus all that you will ever need! He is the well of spiritual, living water!

A second metaphor is "clouds carried by a tempest". These are clouds that seemingly produce nothing. False teachers have nothing to give! The third metaphor is the "blackness of darkness". They lead people to the blackness of hell.

These apostates promote false teaching, are motivated by their own selfish desires and go after those who are not yet grounded in God's word. Follow up and discipleship are primary issues for the family of God. One of the issues of these false prophets is that they seem to have been connected with the gospel but then forsook the truth.

A 'servant of corruption' is not a servant of God! They are in a situation that they enjoy receiving that which should not be theirs! They are not born again servants of God and they lead themselves astray.

Sin looks so good! It promises what it can't produce.

So what is freedom? Freedom is not my way! Freedom is the fulfillment that comes from my relationship to God and the privilege of doing His will. Reformation is without repentance. Repentance leads to the new birth!

The End of False Prophets – II Peter 2:19-22

These false teachers have a very sad end! They may or may not have had an experience. The text seems to indicate that they did. It was not what God's word provides in the new birth. Look at I Peter 1:23-25, *"having been born again, not of corruptible seed but incorruptible, through the word of God which lives and abides forever, because "All flesh is as grass, and all the glory of man as the flower of the grass. The grass withers, and its flower falls away, but the word of the Lord endures forever." Now this is the word which by the gospel was preached to you."* These false teachers may have had knowledge of Christ but there was no change in their life! Their end is tragic. It is worse than the first steps they had when they began down the road! Some Jews called Gentiles 'dogs' and it was a derogatory term. It was a title of disrespect.

Here is an important thing to remember! Satan deceives! He promotes a false gospel. Galatians 1:6-9 says, *"I marvel that you are turning away so soon from Him who called you in the grace of Christ, to a different gospel, which is not another; but there are some who trouble you and want to pervert the gospel of Christ. But even if we, or an angel from heaven, preach any other gospel to you than what we have preached to you, let him be accursed. As we have said before, so now I say again, if anyone preaches any other gospel to you than what you have received, let him be accursed"*. Satan plants false among the true. Matthew 13:34-40 says, *"All these things Jesus spoke to the multitude in parables; and without a parable He did not speak to them, that it might be fulfilled which was spoken by the prophet, saying: "I will open My mouth in parables; I will utter things kept secret from the foundation of the world." Then Jesus sent the multitude away and went into the house. And His disciples came to Him, saying, "Explain to us the parable of the tares of the field." He answered and said to them: "He who sows the good seed is the Son of Man. The field is the world, the good seeds are the sons of the kingdom, but the tares are the sons of the wicked one. The enemy who sowed them is the devil, the harvest is the end of the age, and the reapers are the angels. Therefore as the tares are gathered and burned in the fire, so it will be at the end of this age"*. Peter says a dog is a dog and a pig is a pig! Clean them up on the outside and they are still the same!

To be born again is to become a partaker of the divine nature. Look at II Peter 1:4, *"by which have been given to us exceedingly great and precious promises, that through these you may be partakers of the divine nature, having escaped the corruption that is in the world through lust"*. The question is this. Has our experience with the Lord Jesus been genuine and real? *"Therefore, brethren, be even more diligent to make your call and election sure, for if you do these things you will never stumble"* (II Peter 1:10).

Friends, be careful. Stay away from the counterfeit!

Questions:
1. When did counterfeiting begin?
2. What does pernicious mean?
3. What 3 metaphors does Peter use to describe the empty promises of false prophets?

Discussion:
1. What would be some practical ways to avoid counterfeits in the faith?

Chapter 14

JESUS' COMING IS SURE
II Peter 3:1-16

"Beloved, I now write to you this second epistle (in both of which I stir up your pure minds by way of reminder), that you may be mindful of the words which were spoken before by the holy prophets, and of the commandment of us, the apostles of the Lord and Savior, knowing this first: that scoffers will come in the last days, walking according to their own lusts, and saying, "Where is the promise of His coming? For since the fathers fell asleep, all things continue as they were from the beginning of creation." For this they willfully forget: that by the word of God the heavens were of old, and the earth standing out of water and in the water, by which the world that then existed perished, being flooded with water. But the heavens and the earth which are now preserved by the same word, are reserved for fire until the day of judgment and perdition of ungodly men. But, beloved, do not forget this one thing, that with the Lord one day is as a thousand years, and a thousand years as one day. The Lord is not slack concerning His promise, as some count slackness, but is longsuffering toward us, not willing that any should perish but that all should come to repentance. But the day of the Lord will come as a thief in the night, in which the heavens will pass away with a great noise, and the elements will melt with fervent heat; both the earth and the works that are in it will be burned up." **(II Peter 3:1-16)**

*T*here are constant conversations about the coming of Christ. In the beginning of this book we took the entire chapter on one verse, I Peter 1:13, *"Therefore gird up the loins of your mind, be sober, and rest your hope fully upon the grace that is to be brought to you at the revelation of Jesus Christ."* The coming of the Lord is a theme found throughout Scripture. The apostle Peter in this chapter commences with some important facts concerning the coming of the Lord. He again begins to remind the readers about something important. The word, remember or a form of the word is found throughout II Peter. In verse one he tells readers to be reminded of what they have learned and in verse two he tells them to be mindful of what the prophets and apostles have taught. In the first ten verses there are verses surrounding the coming of the Lord. He speaks to the Scripture (3:1-4), the stability of creation (3:5-7) and the mercy of God (3:8-10).

The Scriptures – II Peter 3:1-4

The Scriptures regularly remind followers of Christ about the Lord's return. The Scriptures are a warning to those who do not follow the Lord of the impending judgment on unbelievers. The day of the Lord is often mentioned in Scripture. The "day of the Lord" is the "day of judgment" that leads to the return of the Lord. I believe there is a rapture preceding the time spoken of as the tribulation. The rapture is of Latin derivation and it refers to the concept of being caught up, taken away. There are other days spoken of in the Bible. For example, II Peter 3:12 states *"looking for and hastening the coming of the day of God, because of which the heavens will be dissolved, being on fire, and the elements will melt with fervent heat."* This day is called the "day of God." It is that time when God's people will be in the new heavens and new earth.

There is also the day of Christ. In I Corinthians 1:7-9 it says, *"so that you come short in no gift, eagerly waiting for the revelation of our Lord Jesus Christ, who will also confirm you to the end, that you may be blameless in the day of our Lord Jesus Christ. God is faithful, by whom you were called into the fellowship of His Son, Jesus Christ our Lord."* *"Holding fast the word of life, so that I may rejoice in the day of Christ that I have not run in vain or labored in vain*" (Philippians 2:16). This day refers to the rapture; the day when Christ comes for His church.

The coming of the Lord is also a time that refers to the impending judgment. Peter writes about many Old Testament prophets who wrote about the "coming of the Lord" and judgment. For example listen to the words of the prophet Isaiah in Isaiah 13:6-16, "*Wail, for the day of the Lord is at hand! It will come as destruction from the Almighty. Therefore all hands will be limp, every man's heart will melt, and they will be afraid. Pangs and sorrows will take hold of them; they will be in pain as a woman in childbirth; they will be amazed at one another; their faces will be like flames. Behold, the day of the Lord comes, cruel, with both wrath and fierce anger, to lay the land desolate; and He will destroy its sinners from it. For the stars of heaven and their constellations will not give their light; the sun will be darkened in its going forth, and the moon will not cause its light to shine. I will punish the world for its evil, and the wicked for their iniquity; I will halt the arrogance of the proud, and will lay low the haughtiness of the terrible. I will make a mortal more rare than fine gold, a man more than the golden wedge of Ophir. Therefore I will shake the heavens, and the earth will move out of her place, in the wrath of the Lord of hosts and in the day of His fierce anger. It shall be as the hunted gazelle, and as a sheep that no man takes up; every man will turn to his own people, and everyone will flee to his own land. Everyone who is found will be thrust through, and everyone who is captured will fall by the sword. Their children also will be dashed to pieces before their eyes; their houses will be plundered and their wives ravished.*"

Daniel writes, "*At that time Michael shall stand up, the great prince who stands watch over the sons of your people; and there shall be a time of trouble, such as never was since there was a nation, even to that time. And at that time your people shall be delivered, everyone who is found written in the book*" (Daniel 12:1). The tribulation period is spoken of as the "time of Jacob's trouble". The time of Jacob's trouble and the tribulation are synonymous in Scripture.

Peter points out that there will be scoffers. A scoffer causes division. A scoffer will mock and ridicule. Now remember in II Peter 2 the apostle is pointing out the false teachers. Mocking the coming of the Lord is at the very heart of their message. ". . .*And especially those who walk according to the flesh in the lust of uncleanness and despise authority. They are presumptuous, self-willed. They are not afraid to speak evil of dignitaries"* (II Peter 2:10). Peter clearly teaches that they allure the weak, contradict the Scriptures and try to minimize any idea of judgment. Notice the promise of these scoffers. They point to the lack of cataclysmic changes in the world. Unbelievably natural catastrophes continue to increase in the world. From Tsunamis to earthquakes to floods and hurricanes the world is rapidly deteriorating.

Stability of the Scriptures – II Peter 3:5-7

Peter suggests to the scoffers two events. Look at the creation and look at the flood. In Genesis one there is the record of God creating the heavens and the earth. He speaks and it occurs. Nine times in the first chapter of the Bible is the phrase "and God said." God spoke and by the command of His edict it occurred! Psalm 19:1-3 reminds us that the heavens and earth creation is found in all of the earth's languages *"The heavens declare the glory of God; and the firmament shows His handiwork. Day unto day utters speech, and night unto night reveals knowledge. There is no speech nor language where their voice is not heard."* Many of the Psalms give great tribute to the creation of the world and contribute this creation to the word of God *"For He spoke, and it was done; He commanded, and it stood fast"* (Psalm 33:9).

Peter's first event is accompanied with an argument. The premise is this: if God spoke the world into existence, He can do whatever He wishes. God spoke and the sun stood still! See in Joshua 10:12-15, *"Then Joshua spoke to the Lord in the day when the Lord delivered up the Amorites before the children of Israel, and he said in the sight of Israel: "Sun, stand still over Gibeon; and Moon, in the Valley of Aijalon." So the sun stood still, and the moon stopped, till the people had revenge upon their enemies. Is this not written in the Book of Jasher? So the sun stood still in the midst of heaven, and did not hasten to go down for about a whole day. And there has been no day like that, before it or after it, that the Lord heeded the voice of a man; for the Lord fought for Israel. Then Joshua returned, and all*

Israel with him, to the camp at Gilgal." When Jesus died there was darkness over all the land in the middle of the day. In Luke 23:44-45 it says, *"Now it was about the sixth hour, and there was darkness over all the earth until the ninth hour. Then the sun was darkened, and the veil of the temple was torn in two."* If God can speak the creation into being, He can certainly intervene with the Lord's return. If He can stop the sun for a day and produce midday darkness over the world when Jesus Christ is accomplishing redemption, He can send the Son of God back at any time.

Peter's second event also is brought with evidences. The flood in Noah's day was a worldwide catastrophic, cataclysmic event. The people who lived in Noah's day were introduced to rain. And my, what a rain it was!

God can do whatever He wants, when He wants. *"But our God is in heaven; He does whatever He pleases"* (Psalm 115:3).

Now Peter begins to drive home the point. In II Peter 3:7 the scripture teaches, *"But the heavens and the earth which are now preserved by the same word, are reserved for fire until the day of judgment and perdition of ungodly men."* God can move, interrupt, speak, start, or stop anything in history because He is God. The term used means, "reserved for time." The verse does not indicate that a human being will destroy the world by nuclear holocaust, but it is God who will burn up the old creation at that moment of time He will bring in the new heavens and earth.

When God created the world, I remind you He spoke it into existence. In Genesis 1, He called it over and over good. At the completion of the sixth day He called it 'very good.' *"Then God saw everything that He had made, and indeed it was very good. So the evening and the morning were the sixth day"* (Genesis 1:31). It is our sin that has brought the curse upon the world. See Romans 8:18-22, *"For I consider that the sufferings of this present time are not worthy to be compared with the glory which shall be revealed in us. For the earnest expectation of the creation eagerly waits for the revealing of the sons of God. For the creation was subjected to futility, not willingly, but because of Him who subjected it in hope; because the creation itself also will be delivered from the bondage of corruption into the glorious liberty of the children of God. For we know that the whole creation groans and labors with birth pangs together until now"* (Romans 8:18-22). Eve and Adam took humanity the wrong way and set the stage for a lost world and the marvelous opportunity for a redeemer! Throughout history mankind has revealed our sinfulness and as environmentalists point out our world is getting polluted. Resources are wasted, oil skyrockets, and frankly the family of the world is facing a crisis.

Mark it down! The Lord Jesus Christ is coming again. Be prepared. When will it happen? No one but the Father knows. We do know why there is a delay. . .

The Longsuffering God – II Peter 3:8-10

Here is a remarkable truth. God sees all things in the eternal present. It is amazing but it is true. *"For a thousand years in Your sight are like yesterday when it is past, and like a watch in the night"* (Psalm 90:4). In God's sight He sees it all. Past, present, and future appears to be in the eternal now with God. What a marvelous God. He is truly an amazing God. God is not limited nor rushed by time or space! The eternality of God is frankly quite amazing. The scripture speaks to the mystery of Godliness. In I Timothy 3:16 it says, *"And without controversy great is the mystery of godliness: God was manifested in the flesh, justified in the Spirit, seen by angels, preached among the Gentiles, believed on in the world, received up in glory."* God is never too late nor too early. God is, in fact, always on time.

God's delay reminds us that He has an awesome plan for the world. He wants sinners to be saved. *"For God so loved the world that He gave His only begotten Son, that whoever believes in Him should not perish but have everlasting life"* (John 3:16). "W*ho desires all men to be saved and to come to the knowledge of the truth"* (I Timothy 2:4). "F*or the Son of Man has come to seek and to save that which was lost"* (Luke 19:10). God has no pleasure in sinners being separated from Him. *"Do I have any pleasure at all that the wicked should die?" says the Lord God, "and not that he should turn from his ways and live?"* (Ezekiel 18:23).

It is interesting to note that God's longsuffering is towards 'us'! There are many views on this but it would appear that the "us' refers to human beings. This could even include the scoffers of the day.

For the first time Peter uses the word 'repentance' in his epistles. In Acts 2:38 in his first sermon (the day of Pentecost message when the Holy Spirit came) he commanded the people to repent. It is somewhat sad that in modern preaching today there are many who do not promote preaching using the word repentance. Jesus was very clear. Jesus said in Luke 13:3,5, *"I tell you, no; but unless you repent you will all likewise perish."* Repentance is not sorrow, remorse, reformation, nor regret. These concepts may be a part of when a person repents. Repentance is not specifically those things. Repentance is a change of the mind that changes a will and it is evidenced by the actions, when a sinner realizes they are lost without a Savior. They will turn from sin to Christ and give their sins to Jesus. In Acts 20:21 it says, *"testifying to Jews, and also to Greeks, repentance toward God and faith toward our Lord Jesus Christ."* In the book of John there are many individuals who came to Jesus and the word believe is often used. In each case the repentance was obvious. Scripture must be compared with scripture. Repentance like grace through faith (Ephesians 2:8-9) is a gift from God. *"When they heard these things they became silent; and they glorified God, saying, "Then God has also granted to the Gentiles repentance to life"* (Acts 11:18). *"In humility correcting those who are in opposition, if God perhaps will grant them repentance, so that they may know the truth"* (II Timothy 2:25).

Peter says we should "come." This is the great invitation. Come to Christ! Come as the song says "just as you are"! It has been my joy in my ministry to lead hundreds of people to Jesus Christ. Often someone will say "I've got to make something right. . ." This may be true but it does not preclude the fact you need to come to Jesus just as you are!

One day our Lord will come again. I do not know when, but He will come. The world will feel everything is all right. Just as a thief does not warn the innocent when he will strike and he will steal from his victims, our Lord will come! See I Thessalonians 5:3, *"For when they say, "peace and safety!" then sudden destruction comes upon them, as labor pains upon a pregnant woman. And they shall not escape."*

Peter completes this passage with a warning again using the term "the day of the Lord". In II Peter 3:10 it says, *"But the day of the Lord will come as a thief in the night, in which the heavens will pass away with a great noise, and the elements will melt with fervent heat; both the earth and the works that are in it will be burned up."* The word dissolved refers to something broken down in its basic elements as it says in Matthew 24:35, *"Heaven and earth will pass away, but My words will by no means pass away."* God is making room for the new heaven and the new earth.

Not long ago my wife and I saved our money and bought with cash a beautiful Toyota Highlander automobile. It had all the bells and whistles that a fine car is to have. I travel about 50 weekends every year preaching in churches and numerous other weekdays to speak with pastors, leaders, and Bible Conferences. This vehicle was to be our auto for these trips. In a manner of a few weeks we were traveling on Route 220 south in Pennsylvania to speak in a church and a deer decided to test the strength of our new Highlander. The whole right front of this beautiful auto showed the damage. So many things we have and work hard for are quickly damaged or destroyed. My friend, don't live for things. Live knowing that our dear Lord is coming!

Preparing for a New Day – II Peter 3:11-18

"Therefore, since all these things will be dissolved, what manner of persons ought you to be in holy conduct and godliness, looking for and hastening the coming of the day of God, because of which the heavens will be dissolved, being on fire, and the elements will melt with fervent heat? Nevertheless we, according to His promise, look for new heavens and a new earth in which righteousness dwells. Therefore, beloved, looking forward to these things, be diligent to be found by Him in peace, without spot and blameless; and consider that the longsuffering of our Lord is salvation—as also our beloved brother Paul, according to the wisdom given to him, has written to you, as also in all his epistles, speaking in them of these things, in which are some things hard to understand, which untaught and unstable people twist to their own destruction, as they do also the rest of the Scriptures. You therefore, beloved, since you know this

beforehand, beware lest you also fall from your own steadfastness, being led away with the error of the wicked; but grow in the grace and knowledge of our Lord and Savior Jesus Christ. To Him be the glory both now and forever. Amen."

All Christians believe that Jesus Christ is coming back. Prophecy should motivate every follower of Christ. Our motivation is based on several key factors. One of them is the blessed promise of our Lord's return. The return of the Lord should motivate us and the final verses of II Peter give us three motivations. The first is to:

Live Godly Lives – II Peter 3:11-14

Peter encourages us to be eager, to look with great anticipation. I am a grandfather and when I know the grandchildren are coming to our home it is with eagerness I look for them. What excitement when they jump into Grandpa's arms. I want to be a good grandfather for them. Peter teaches that since the Lord is coming we are all to be in holiness and conduct expecting the Lord's return. Verse 12 teaches we are to look for the coming of the Lord. The word is described "as expectancy". It describes excitement, anticipation, and expectancy. Since this world as we know it, will be dissolved, we look with great expectancy to the coming of the Lord. It is possible that Christians can get disillusioned or distracted and even become lukewarm but the immediacy of Christ's coming will prompt us to eagerly look for our Lord with expectancy. Frankly there are times when I simply wish Jesus would come. It is imperative to remember the precious promises of our Lord. This is one that is so vital. Jesus Christ is coming again! Verse 11 speaks about the "manner" to live. The word is from a root word that speaks to the thought of foreign. I have traveled to numerous places in the world. As a foreigner, I am the guest. The place where I am visiting is not my home. Likewise in this world we are heading toward another place. We are reminded by Peter in I Peter 2:11, *"Beloved, I beg you as sojourners and pilgrims, abstain from fleshly lusts which war against the soul."* We are called to holiness. The word means separate. We as followers of Christ are called out and separated unto Him. The word godliness means that followers of Christ worship the Lord and are devoted to Him. There are numerous passages that teach us about purity. *"But concerning the times and the seasons, brethren, you have no need that I should write to you. For you yourselves know perfectly that the day of the Lord so comes as a thief in the night. For when they say, "peace and safety!" then sudden destruction comes upon them, as labor pains upon a pregnant woman. And they shall not escape. But you, brethren, are not in darkness, so that this day should over-take you as a thief. You are all sons of light and sons of the day. We are not of the night nor of darkness. Therefore let us not sleep, as others do, but let us watch and be sober. For those who sleep, sleep at night, and those who get drunk are drunk at night. But let us who are of the day be sober, putting on the breastplate of faith and love, and as a helmet the hope of salvation. For God did not appoint us to wrath, but to obtain salvation through our Lord Jesus Christ, who died for us, that whether we wake or sleep, we should live together with Him. Therefore comfort each other and edify one another, just as you also are doing"* (I Thessalonians 5:1-11). When the apostle Paul was dying, he spoke of "loving the Lord's appearing". In II Timothy 4:8 it says, *"Finally, there is laid up for me the crown of righteousness, which the Lord, the righteous Judge, will give to me on that day, and not to me only but also to all who have loved His appearing"*.

The phrase "looking for and hastening the coming of the day of God" is interesting. Do we as Christians actually hurry the coming of the Lord? What does this mean? Warren Wiersbe in his excellent teaching on II Peter teaches that the word 'hasten' occurs in five other passages. *"And they came with haste and found Mary and Joseph, and the Babe lying in a manger"* (Luke 2:16). The shepherds were to hasten to see the Christ child. Jesus commanded Zaccheus to "make haste". Remember he was in the tree and Jesus was about to change the life of this tax collector. See Acts 20:16, *" For Paul had decided to sail past Ephesus, so that he would not have to spend time in Asia; for he was hurrying to be at Jerusalem, if possible, on the Day of Pentecost."* And Acts 22:18, *"and saw Him saying to me, 'make haste and get out of Jerusalem quickly, for they will not receive your testimony concerning Me."* This word can be used as a synonym for eager anticipation.

So how do we hasten the coming of the Lord? We are taught to pray in Matthew 6:10, *"Your kingdom come. Your will be done on earth as it is in heaven."* Jesus is calling out a people unto Himself. We are to serve and be faithful. Jesus is coming. One day the last sinner will be saved. We shall then see Him! This earth will be dissolved and we can see our Lord! Be faithful child of God! We need to keep this promise in our hearts. We are to be waiting and anticipate the Lord's return.

Lead Sinners to Christ – II Peter 3:15-16

Peter now refers to his good friend, the apostle Paul. Paul wrote of many deep truths in scripture. Ephesians is a marvelous presentation of what God has done for us and then how we are to live out our lives. Ephesians 1-3 describes the doctrine of our faith and chapters 4-6 present how we should live out our faith. Paul taught us through divine inspiration the truth of Jew and Gentile coming into the family of God.

Peter speaks about unlearned and unstable people. We live in a day when there is very little understanding or grasping of a Biblical worldview because people do not understand the Bible. I have the honor of being the president of a college that is thoroughly committed to a Biblical worldview. We are on a journey to pursue God and to learn His word. False teaching is best characterized by taking snippets of scripture, pulling them out of context and teaching them as truth. We teach our young preachers to know the text of scripture before making applications.

The warning here is very clear. Those who twist and distort the scriptures do so "unto their own destruction". The word destruction has become common with Peter. (II Peter 2:1-3; 3:7; 3:16) *"But there were also false prophets among the people, even as there will be false teachers among you, who will secretly bring in destructive heresies, even denying the Lord who bought them, and bring on themselves swift destruction. And many will follow their destructive ways, because of whom the way of truth will be blasphemed. By covetousness they will exploit you with deceptive words; for a long time their judgment has not been idle, and their destruction does not slumber."*) *"But the heavens and the earth which are now preserved by the same word, are reserved for fire until the day of judgment and perdition of ungodly men.* " (3:16) *"as also in all his epistles, speaking in them of these things, in which are some things hard to understand, which untaught and unstable people twist to their own destruction, as they do also the rest of the Scriptures."* It speaks to damnation. It is a tragic eternity separated from God.

We need to win people to Jesus Christ. Soul winning, evangelism, and personal witnessing are mandatory for believers. We are living in the post modern era. In the pre modern era there was the preaching of some of history's greatest preachers. This was the era when proclamation is what expounded truth. Then there was the modern era. The modern era is best described by defending the truth. The great Darrow/Bryon debates characterized this era. The major issue was creationism versus evolution. In post modernism the need is to live the truth. It is not that proclaiming the truth and debating truth is not necessary but if that truth isn't lived then the truth will not have a listening ear!

Grow In Knowledge – II Peter 3:17-18

Twice in the final two verses of II Peter the apostle mentions the importance of know. He reminds us to ". . .know this beforehand. . ." and to ". . .grow in the grace and knowledge. . ." the first of these emphasize a knowledge to beware of falling from your own steadfastness. The word "beware" is a reference to guarding the truth and living by the truth of God's word. Knowledge of the truth mentally can actually lead to pride. Pride leads to overconfidence. This will lead to a fall. Living the truth is based on knowledge of the faith but faith that is mental ascent is not the faith changing our lives. *"Wherefore let him that thinketh he standeth take heed lest he fall"* (I Corinthians 10:12). The danger is that false teachers would lead people astray. He calls this the "error of the wicked". The word wicked has a root meaning that refers to the lawless. Again Peter's emphasize is on those who proclaim freedom without responsibility. (II Peter 2:10-11; 2:19) *"and especially those who walk according to the flesh in the lust of uncleanness and despise authority. They are presumptuous, self-willed. They are not afraid to speak evil of dignitaries, whereas angels, who are greater in power and might, do not bring a reviling accusation against them before the Lord.*" *(2:19) "While they promise them liberty, they themselves are slaves of corruption; for by whom a person is overcome, by him also he is brought into bondage.*"

Salvation is eternal. Yet, he talks here about steadfastness. In II Peter 1:12 it says, *"For this reason I will not be negligent to remind you always of these things, though you know and are established in the present truth."* The steadfastness he refers to is the stability that the word of God gives us. When there is a new convert, the new babe in Christ needs to be in a place of spiritual growth. Years ago, Robert Raikes saw this need and began the Sunday School Movement. The small group ministry of many churches connects young believers with spiritual people who want to grow. Young converts need careful direction. Peter has reminded his readers that when someone accepts Jesus Christ as their Savior there are those who try to bring them into their fold! *"For when they speak great swelling words of emptiness, they allure through the lusts of the flesh, through lewdness, the ones who have actually escaped from those who live in error"* (II Peter 2:18).

As a young pastor I was invited to speak at a Bible conference with Dr. Lehman Strauss. Dr. Strauss was a popular and beloved conference speaker. It was an honor to speak with him. At lunch I asked him for advice he could give to a young preacher. He quickly responded. The essence of what he said was: "Learn the doctrines of the Bible with brief one sentence definitions. Memorize them." That was one of the best pieces of advice I received. Likewise young believers need to know the doctrines of God's word. Then there needs to be follow up concerning how to 'live out' the faith. Verse 18 reminds believers to grow and the meaning is to "constantly grow." Our spiritual walk should be consistent and growing. This growth must be in grace.

God's riches at Christ's expense should regularly be on our mind. But grace in salvation is simply the beginning. Ephesians 2:8-9 states, *"For by grace you have been saved through faith, and that not of yourselves; it is the gift of God, [9] not of works, lest anyone should boast."* These are oft quoted verses but verse ten gives us the reason they are so important. *"For we are His workmanship, created in Christ Jesus for good works, which God prepared before-hand that we should walk in them"* (Ephesians 2:10). Grace is there-fore for service.

Grace also strengthens our lives. *"You therefore, my son, be strong in the grace that is in Christ Jesus. And the things that you have heard from me among many witnesses, commit these to faithful men who will be able to teach others also. You therefore must endure hardship as a good soldier of Jesus Christ. No one engaged in war-fare entangles himself with the affairs of this life, that he may please him who enlisted him as a soldier"* (II Timothy 2:1-4). Truly we can repeat what Peter said earlier in the epistle, *"But may the God of all grace, who called us to His eternal glory by Christ Jesus, after you have suffered a while, perfect, establish, strengthen, and settle you"* (I Peter 5:10). In I Peter 4:10, Peter writes, *"As each one has received a gift, minister it to one another, as good stewards of the manifold grace of God."* As we journey through life it is God's grace that we follow. The end of the story of our journey is that we are to become more Christ like.

To grow in grace means we are to increase knowledge. Knowledge and grace go hand in hand together as we mature. The purpose is to grow "in the knowledge of our Lord and Savior, Jesus Christ". Knowledge alone puffs up. We are to become like Christ in our journey with Him.

The local church is a major instrument that God uses. We are side by side with believers who are experiencing their journey of faith. We share with each other and therefore grow together.

The result of this growth is the glory of God. God's glory is eternal. Glory is all that God is. Glory is not an attribute of God but it is the sum total of all that God is. An old time preacher, Dr. James M. Grey, once expressed life this way in one of his songs, "who can mind the journey, when the road leads home?"

Jesus is coming back. All glory belongs to Him. This may be the day of His return but if it is not, followers of Jesus can still say, "All glory belongs to Him!"

Questions

1. What are the lessons you have learned from this volume and how can you apply them to your life?
2. What is meant in Scripture by the glory of God?

Epilogue

*I*n the beginning of this book I mentioned some things about the life of Peter. History speaks of several important Peters. Peter the Great was the Russian Czar between 1682-1725 A.D. Peter II was a King 1934-45. The best known Peter is the apostle. What a unique man. He appears to be the ultimate of the sanguine personality. He was the man who hit the proverbial ball out of the park! He was the one who declared who Jesus was (Matthew 16:16-18). He alone walked on water to Jesus. He also struck out. It was also Peter who initially refused to allow Jesus to wash his feet. He proclaimed he would defend and die for Jesus only to deny Him before a little slave girl. Yet it was Peter, who when filled by the Holy Spirit, gave one of the most remarkable messages of church history, the Day of Pentecost message (Acts 2). Peter was confronted by Paul when he began to move away from the message of God's grace and it was Peter who wrote this epistle. I personally believe that a proper understanding of the divinely inspired epistle needs an understanding of the man's life.

He was a man with three names. His given name was Simon. It was our Lord who changed it to Peter which means a stone (John 1:35-42). The Aramaic meaning of Peter is Cephas.

Many historians set the time of Paul's death around A.D. 64. These epistles were probably written around 63-64 A.D. Probably later that year Peter died. Tradition teaches he died a death of crucifixion and requested to be crucified upside down on the cross because he was not worthy to be crucified like his Lord. The old hymn said it so well, "Hallelujah, what a Savior". I suppose if Peter were here he would want us to say less of him and more or his Savior. The fact is, however, his legacy lives on! The testimony of my good friend and a trustee of Davis College, Mike Houlihan, bears witness. . .

Michael H. Houlihan:
Personal Testimony for
1 and 2 Peter Commentary

I am especially thankful for the apostle Peter because he was the primary instrument the Lord used to lead me to salvation. I was raised a Roman Catholic in a devout and loving, religious home. Soon after entering college, I abandoned my religion for all the world had to offer. On several occasions in my life, sincere Christians had shared with me their faith in Jesus Christ and what it meant to be "born again." From their testimony I understood that I was a sinner and that the gift of the salvation of my soul would be accomplished if I placed my faith in Jesus Christ alone as my personal Savior. Obviously, this was great news, but I wasn't convinced that Christ could give me that gift because I wasn't convinced that He had actually risen from the dead. At that point in my life, Jesus was simply a great teacher with a love for mankind, but not God the Son who died and rose from the dead to pay the penalty for my sin.

I was educated and prospering as a successful businessman, but I wasn't "happy" with all of the things the world had promised would bring me happiness. That "emptiness" prompted a search for meaning in my life which led to studying the four Gospels. Reading the life of Christ left me even more skeptical of Jesus' resurrection from the dead. The Bible relates that despite many miracles to substantiate His credentials as the Messiah, all of His followers denied any association with Him at His public crucifixion. The Bible records that the apostle Peter, whom Jesus had appointed as the leader of the apostles, denied Jesus three times. The last time Peter even denied Him with a curse.

My search for proof of the resurrection in the Bible had pretty much ended until one night in the local public library. While searching for another book, I came across a book which was mis-filed on the library bookshelves. It was a book on the lives of the apostles. I know now that the Lord had sovereignly placed that book there for me. I turned to the life of the apostle Peter and discovered that he had died a martyr's death under the persecutions of the Roman emperor Nero. Confronted with recanting his faith in Jesus Christ to save his life, the apostle Peter refused, and requested that he be crucified upside down. History records that the apostle Peter told his executioners that he was "unworthy to die the way Jesus died" and he wanted to be crucified upside down.

There among the bookshelves in the library, secular history's indelible record shocked my sensibilities. Why was Peter now giving up his life for Jesus? Why not deny Christ as he did at the cross? What could possibly have happened after the crucifixion to change Peter's mind to die for Christ? Obviously, Peter was not now afraid of death. Something had happened that convinced Peter that he had eternal life.

History records that Peter and all of the other apostles except John died martyr's deaths, proclaiming that they had seen Jesus risen from the dead and they had watched Him ascend into heaven. Do men give up their lives for a lie? Peter's change of behavior and martyrdom established for me the truth of Jesus' resurrection from the dead. Peter was not afraid to die because he had watched Jesus die on the cross and had seen Him alive resurrected from the dead. Peter sealed the truth of his testimony with his own blood. In the local public library, God graciously saved my soul, and through Peter, revealed the truth of the resurrection of the Lord Jesus Christ. Peter's blood, and that of all of those eyewitnesses of Jesus' crucifixion and resurrection, defies any other explanation for their change of faith and martyrdom. Jesus of Nazareth lives . . . He is the Christ of God!

CPSIA information can be obtained at www.ICGtesting.com
Printed in the USA
BVOW080736081112

304956BV00001B/6/P